INVOKE A BLESSING

ON YOURSELF

Yuri I. Tereshchenko

Invoke A Blessing On Yourself.

Copyright 2010 by Yuri I. Tereshchenko
All rights reserved. Written permission must be secured from the publisher to reproduce or use any part of this book, except for brief quotations.
All scriptures are in King James Version unless specified.
Scripture quotations marked The Message Bible are taken from THE MESSAGE: The Bible in Contemporary Language © 2002 by Eugene H. Peterson. All rights reserved.
Scriptures quotations marked AMP are taken from The Amplified Bible...
Scriptures quotations marked NKJV are taken from The Holy Bible, The New King James Version...
CEV is Contemporary English Version.

Contemporary English Version®
Copyright © 1995 American Bible Society. All rights reserved.

Bible text from the Contemporary English Version (CEV) is not to be reproduced in copies or otherwise by any means except as permitted in writing by American Bible Society, 1865 Broadway, New York, NY 10023 (www.americanbible.org).

Scripture quotations marked (TLB) are taken from The Living Bible copyright © 1971. Used by permission of Tyndale House Publishers, Inc., Wheaton, IL 60189. All rights reserved.

Published in Ft. Worth, Texas, by Yuri I. Tereshchenko
Tereshchenko, Yuri 1978 –
Printed in the United States of America

Invoke A Blessing On Yourself.

Contents

Foreword	8
Appreciation	12
Dedication	14
Why I Wrote This Book	19
1. Do You Read To Understand The Bible… Or Do You Read To Defend Your Preconceived Knowledge?	24
2. Did You Know The World Needs You?	31
3. Where Did This All Begin?	36
4. God Wants You To Be Blessed	46

Invoke A Blessing On Yourself.

5. How Committed Are You To Changing Things In Your Life?	50
6. How About A Friend… For A Change?	58
7. Are You Abiding By The Law?	64
8. Are You Ready For Your Miracle Experience	70
9. Are You Ready To Predict Your Future?	78
10. You Too Can Create Your Own Future	84
11. It's Not The How, It's When…!	90
12. Why Did Abraham Have To Change His Name?	96

Invoke A Blessing On Yourself.

13. Choose Faith And Strength; Reject Fear And Unbelief — 102

14. Decree A Thing And It Shall Be Established Unto You — 108

15. Your Children Are A Heritage From The Lord — 116

16. A Willing Heart — 124

17. Honor — 128

18. Excellence — 136

19. Deception Is Not Beneficial For Your Health...Or For Your Future Success... — 142

Invoke A Blessing On Yourself.

20. What You Know And What You Do Not Know	148
21. Sow Into Your Future	154
22. Finances	162
23. Do You Have The Attitude of A Giant or A Grasshopper?	168
24. Whose Voice Have You Chosen To Listen To?	176
25. Always Listen To And Listen For The Voice of The Holy Spirit	182

Invoke A Blessing On Yourself.

26. Why Job Got What He Really, Really Did Not Want?   192

27. You Are The Commander of Your Destiny, The Master of Your Ship   198

28. Have You Ever Lost What You Had Already Gained?   204

29. Invoke A Blessing Or A Curse   208

30. The Blessing Will Reside In Your Thoughts... And In Your Mind   214

31. Do Not Peck Like A Chicken...Soar Like An Eagle   220

Invoke A Blessing On Yourself.

32. Nurture And Develop Worthwhile Relationships   224

33. The Proverbs 31 Woman   230

34. In Conclusion...   244

Invoke Salvation On Yourself   246

Prayer To Receive The Gift of The Holy Spirit   247

Invoke A Blessing On Yourself.

Foreword by Dr. Harold Herring.

Have you ever been on a delightful trip? One filled with moments of "oooh" and "aahh?" Memories that fired your imagination . . . stirred your spirit and made you want to visit those locations time and time again?

You're about to undertake such a journey as you turn the pages of <u>Invoke A Blessing On Yourself</u> by my dear friend, Yuri Tereshchenko.

Yuri's story is one of desire, dedication and determination to overcome every adversity while achieving the success He knows God created for every believer to enjoy.

But there is only one way to read this anointed book. . .with a pen and paper in hand . . . or more preferable, with an electronic notepad because you'll want to refer to your notes again and again.

I have read over this manuscript several times and each time, I find myself stopping to write down thoughts and ideas God stirs in me as I turn the pages.

Invoke A Blessing On Yourself.

This book is not just a story of faith. . .it's a "how to" manual for bringing God's richest blessings into your life . . . right now ... today.

<u>Invoke A Blessing On Yourself</u> is inspirational, motivational and rich with revelatory insight. But it's much, much more. It is filled with practical strategies for improving the quality of your life and those you love.

I know you too will find yourself moved by the faith of the Tereshchenko family to achieve wisdom, health and wealth.

You will be blessed by how they stood in faith for Nadia's healing after being swarmed by fire ants. Page after page is loaded with insight and antidotes that will ignite your desire to live this faith-filled life.

I'm an avid reader and for eight of the past ten years I've read a book a week authored by many people whom I didn't know. I've read stories but I truthfully couldn't tell you if they practiced what they preached.

I know Yuri. . .he is exactly the kind of man that his book portrays. He exemplifies a spiritual maturity far beyond his natural years.

Invoke A Blessing On Yourself.

He is devoted to his beautiful wife, Nadia, and his precious children, Deonna and Simon with a passion befitting any model of husband and father. I also know from personal experience that he knows how to honor and serve and be a friend to those who need one.

As you begin your journey through this book. . . you will find your life enriched, your faith strengthened, your heart encouraged and your horizons broadened.

There is one last thing. Before you ever read the last page of this book, you'll realize you can experience a success in life you never thought possible. And you'll have Yuri Tereshchenko to thank for that.

Harold Herring

President

Debt Free Army

Rich Thoughts TV

Invoke A Blessing On Yourself.

I Don't Have A Thing God Didn't Give Me... And I Don't Want To Invoke A Thing God Doesn't Want Me To Have.

-Yuri I. Tereshchenko

Invoke A Blessing On Yourself.

APPRECIATION

First of all, I thank The Father, The Son and The Holy Spirit for my life. The unforgettable revelation that The Holy Spirit gave me *prompted* and *guided* me in the writing of this book. Thank You, Holy Spirit, for always being beside me. Thank You for teaching me that without you I would not be who I am…

Dear Dr. Mike Murdock, thank you for your love and mentorship. Thank you for encouraging us to *write* a book. When I got the revelation, I thought to myself, if Dr. Murdock has written over 300 books, surely I can get *one* book out. Thank you, Dr. Mike Murdock, for imparting the wisdom and knowledge that we need to live *successfully* on the earth. Thank you for your articulate delivery and crystal clear communication of the message of God's plan and purpose for our lives. It is because of your ministry we were led to stop what we were doing in Nebraska and move to Dallas/Ft. Worth. It has been said, "Everything is bigger in Texas." The Wisdom you teach is *big* to me and my family…

Much appreciation goes out to Dr. Harold and Pastor Beverly Herring. Both of you have been a *great* source of motivation and encouragement as I worked on this book project. My wife and I are thankful for the time

Invoke A Blessing On Yourself.

you have invested into our lives. Thank you for teaching and mentoring us. Thank you for your relationship and friendship with us. We *treasure* your investment into our lives. Thank you, Dr. Harold, for writing the Foreword to *Invoke A Blessing On Yourself*. It is with great Honor that I receive your endorsement of this book.

I appreciate Pastors Carlos and Gabriella Lira for sowing a very generous seed into our ministry to help publish this book. Thank you for your friendship dear Pastors Carlos and Gabriella. Thank you for your prayers and financial support. I and my wife value your friendship.

My appreciation goes out to Mr. Paul Nyamweya for diligently editing this book and bringing your experience and expertise into making every page come alive...and for keeping the readers focused on the message in the book. *Thank you, sir.*

Invoke A Blessing On Yourself.

DEDICATION

As a husband, father and friend, I want to dedicate my first book, *Invoke a Blessing on Yourself*, to the three most *important* people in my life.

They *motivate* me to wake up very early, *every* morning, and spend time with The Holy Spirit, as I prepare to face each new day as a *champion*...and not a *chump*. They *challenge* me to stay up late and get things done. They *encourage* me to stay focused.

They are one of the reasons I wrote this book.

They are one of the reasons I never give up or quit.

They are one of the reasons I stay *persistent*.

As a breadwinner, I want to produce and take good care of my family, who are the three most *important* humans in my life.

My *first* dedication is to my wife, Nadia. You believe in *me* and in my *dreams*. You never criticize my ideas or my dreams, but you pray for me; and as The Lord gives you instructions, only then do you offer your input.

Thank you for being a great friend and partner.

Invoke A Blessing On Yourself.

Thank you for your faithfulness and your loyalty. I will love you forever. You are the *only* one for me. My mother did not raise a fool; we have made it this far. I will be forever yours.

The *second* most important human in my life is our daughter Deonna. You are my *princess*. I will never forget the *moment* you were born. I was there to cut the umbilical cord. When you would wake up in the middle of the night, I would get up to help your mother.

About a month, after you were born, we dedicated you to The Lord. During the dedication, a prophesy was spoken by the pastor that you would be a dancer and worshiper. You are the *best* dancer and worshiper that I know. I will *always* love you; my princess and my friend.

The *third* most important human in my life is my son, Simon. I was there when you were born, even though I almost passed out. When you were little, I would get up most nights to make sure you and your sister were covered with a blanket. I made sure the home was secure.

I will never forget when we got called to the front of the church, in Omaha, Nebraska. Your mother was holding you in her arms as Reverend Mary Francis Varrallo prophesied over us.

She asked, "Who are you people? God's hand is upon you and I see you travelling." Then she turned to

Invoke A Blessing On Yourself.

you Simon and said, "You look like a Tzar. You are going to be a great one."

Son, now that I see you growing up, I know you will be a *champion*. That is why I call you "Champ." You have a *kind* heart. You *always* want to do the *right* thing. You are never afraid to apologize when you make a mistake, because you *want* to be a blessing.

You are going to bless *many* people, because of your success. You have integrity. I will be your best friend *forever*. I will help you succeed. I love you, Champ!

In conclusion, when my parents decided to immigrate to The United States of America, they had a dream. Their dream was to live in a country where people could *freely* serve God. Their desire was to live in a nation where the government would not *restrict* them from taking their children to church *before* they turned eighteen years old.

In Ukraine, if you did not comply with this law, the government *threatened* you with the loss of your children. After my parents made the decision to move, we lived, breathed and dreamt about being in The United States of America. We had such strong conviction that *nothing* in the world could *stop* us from achieving it.

If you purpose to accomplish something with such a *passion* that you are *unable* to live with failure, you will

Invoke A Blessing On Yourself.

eventually achieve it, as long as it does not contradict The Bible.

You…and any one…can *achieve* it.

Yes, you can *Invoke A Blessing On Yourself*.

Invoke A Blessing On Yourself.

> *Invoke A Blessing On Yourself By Attracting It And Letting It Come To You As A Fisherman Would... Instead of Chasing After It As A Hunter.*
>
> *-Yuri I. Tereshchenko*

"And He saith unto them, Follow Me, and I will make you fishers of men," (Matthew 4:19).

Invoke A Blessing On Yourself.

Why I Wrote This Book.

The title and purpose of this book came to me as I was praying in The Spirit. The Holy Spirit gave me a revelation of Isaiah 65:16 (AMP). "So it shall be that he who invokes a blessing on himself in the land shall do so by saying, May the God of truth and fidelity [the Amen] bless me; and he who takes an oath in the land shall swear by the God of truth and faithfulness to His promises [the Amen], because the former troubles are forgotten and because they are hidden from My eyes."

In the 2010 Online Merriam-Webster's Dictionary, Invoke stands for:
1 to petition for help or support
2 to call forth : CONJURE
3 to make an earnest request for : SOLICIT
4 to put into effect or operation : IMPLEMENT
5 BRING ABOUT, CAUSE
— in·vok·er *noun*

Even as God, our Father, spoke the world into existence, you too can use biblical principles to *frame* the world that you and your family live in.

Invoke A Blessing On Yourself.

This book will *help* you if you apply these principles. This book will *change* your life if you will fully *embrace* these principles. Your life will never be the same if you carefully read through and study this book. Read it over and over again. The Bible promises, "Anything is possible to the one who believes." (See Mark 9:23.)

> I Want To Provoke And Guide You To Invoke And Keep The Blessing On Your Life.
>
> -Yuri I. Tereshchenko

This is not a book about sitting passively and *waiting* for God to deliver to you what you need. This book will challenge you to use your faith to *attract* what God has already declared for you to receive. May you speak into existence all The Blessings God has intended for you to possess. May you never, through doubt-filled words, repudiate The Blessings God has purposed for you to receive. May you develop an understanding of the principles that have been in The Bible for thousands of years. May you master silencing doubt and unbelief, while *activating* your faith.

The Bible says, "But without faith it is impossible to please Him," (Hebrews 11:6). The lack of faith may be one of the reasons you have not been as successful as you

Invoke A Blessing On Yourself.

desire to be. You must *use* your faith to have an *uncommon* Future.

Jesus invoked a blessing on the *children*. "And He took them up in His arms, put His hands upon them, and blessed them," (Mark 10:16).

Jesus invoked blessing upon *enemies*. "Bless them that curse you, and pray for them which despitefully use you," (Luke 6:28).

Jesus invoked a blessing on *His disciples*. "And He led them out as far as to Bethany, and He lifted up His hands, and blessed them," (Luke 24:50).

> You Will Invoke Success If You Are Success-Conscious; You Will Invoke Failure If You Are Failure-Conscious.
>
> -Yuri I. Tereshchenko

The principle of *invoking a blessing on yourself* will affect the favor on your life, your success, your health, your finances, your job, your family and even your spiritual success. You will only succeed in the areas you *focus* on. You will get what you think about *most* of the time. You will become the kind of person you imagine you are. "For as he thinketh in his heart, so is he," (Proverbs 23:7).

Invoke A Blessing On Yourself.

Are You Success-Conscious Or Failure-Conscious?

You will live into the *picture* you have conceived in your *mind*. Henry Ford said: "If you think you can or if you think you can't, you are right."

Success comes to those who are *success-conscious*.

Failure comes to those who are *failure-conscious*.

You will keep failing if you keep thinking about failure and you will keep succeeding if you keep thinking about success. The Art of Receiving is based on how *success-conscious* you are.

In this book you will learn how to invoke success-consciousness. You will learn The Art of Receiving. You will learn how to *keep* and *protect* the blessings bestowed upon your life. You will discover how to *train* your children, how to be a *strong* Christian and how to *hear* The Voice of The Holy Spirit. This book contains the secrets to *having, being* or *doing* anything using biblical principles.

All the wonderful sermons and teachings you have heard and read are golden pieces to a *big* puzzle. This book will show you how to put the pieces of the puzzle together and envision the masterpiece that The Bible is conveying to each believer.

All the faith messages you have hidden in your heart are going to come alive and open up like a big

Invoke A Blessing On Yourself.

beautiful flower, and you will see the BIG picture of what God has promised to us in His Word.

God sent His Son, but he left us His Book...*The Bible*. As you read your Bible, you will see *golden* nuggets throughout the scriptures that you and I need to apply to *experience* and *live* The Blessed Life. If you follow The Laws and The Principles of The Bible, you can *invoke a blessing on yourself*.

Invoke A Blessing On Yourself.

1

Do You Read To Understand The Bible...Or Do You Read To Defend Your Preconceived Knowledge?

The Bible contains life principles.

I will go through The Bible using some of the examples of what I have experienced. When *applied*, the principles will make you *successful* in all aspects of your life. God wants us blessed. He gave us His Word so we could learn how to *invoke* His blessing, *keep* His blessing and *spread* His blessing to others by sowing Seeds of faith.

Invoke A Blessing On Yourself.

When you help others, you are sowing a Seed for your Future. "Knowing that whatsoever good thing any man doeth, the same shall he receive of the Lord, whether he be bond or free," (Ephesians 6:8).

As you become more and more blessed, you will become *capable* of blessing others even more. Remember that *whatsoever* you say, whether positive or negative, you will get. "A man shall eat good by the fruit of his mouth," (Proverbs 13:2).

Name your Future and *claim* your blessings.

Whatever Is Missing In Your Life...Is Something You Do Not Yet Know How To Invoke On Yourself.

-Yuri I. Tereshchenko

Don't be a fool; God *wants* you to have an uncommon life. God wants you *blessed*! "Fear not, little flock; for it is your Father's good pleasure to give you the kingdom," (Luke 12:32). "Beloved, I wish above all things that thou mayest prosper and be in health, even as thy soul prospereth," (3 John 2).

The world will tell you otherwise, yet wealthy people have *prospered* financially because they applied *biblical* principles, either knowingly or unknowingly. You can and you will be blessed *beyond* your imagination if

Invoke A Blessing On Yourself.

you only *learn* and *master* the simple principles of The Bible. Can you stand to be blessed?! I must warn you that if you want to learn and understand these principles, you have to read these pages with *open* mind.

You must be *teachable*. As soon as you say, "Oh! I already know that," you *hinder* your learning capacity and your growth. The reason you have not been as successful as you want to be, or had the things you wanted to have, is because there is *something* you do not know.

In fact, you do not know what you do not know.

It is with this mindset that I will encourage you to read this book.

My Experience.

I was raised in a Baptist church.
We *read* The Bible.
We *sang* about The Bible.
We *preached* from The Bible.
We *quoted* The Bible.
We tried to always *live* by The Bible.

The theology I was taught as a young believer *molded* my beliefs. My beliefs *influenced* what I preached at my father's church and other Baptist churches that I travelled to and ministered in.

My persuasions since then have *radically* changed.

Invoke A Blessing On Yourself.

There were a lot of things in The Bible that were not taught or talked about in my former church. As a result, I had never seen them for myself before. After I was enlightened, my reading and understanding of The Bible became *different*.

Studying The Bible became more *interesting*.

I had discovered the *gold*. "The statutes of the Lord are right, rejoicing the heart: the commandment of the Lord is pure, enlightening the eyes. The fear of the Lord is clean, enduring for ever: the judgments of the Lord are true and righteous altogether. More to be desired are they than gold, yea, than much fine gold: sweeter also than honey and the honeycomb," (Psalm 19:8-10).

From then on, I knew my life would *never* be the same. It was as if a whole *new* world had opened up for me. Now that I am full of The Holy Spirit, with evidence of speaking in tongues, a lot of things have *changed*.

I have received new revelation about Faith, Divine Healing, Prosperity, Wisdom, etc.

Reading And Understanding The Bible.

Many people read The Bible with *preconceived* knowledge, instead of reading to *understand*. Many read with a *set* understanding because that was the way it was taught or presented to them.

Invoke A Blessing On Yourself.

What do I mean by that?

I will give you *several* examples. In The Gospel of Mark, The Bible documents Jesus raising a little girl from the dead. "And He took the damsel by the hand, and said unto her, Talitha cumi; which is, being interpreted, Damsel, I say unto thee, arise," (Mark 5:41).

If they all spoke Hebrew why would He use a *different* language? Nowhere in The Bible does it say that Jesus sometimes spoke a different language. Were there times they had to find an interpreter to translate what He said. No! They never did *need* interpretation.

Those words were not accurately translated because no one is absolutely sure what those words *really* meant. We can call it an *assumptive* interpretation.

A *second* example is found in the book of Mark, when Jesus was hanging on The Cross. "And at the ninth hour Jesus cried with a loud voice, saying, Eloi, Eloi, lama sabachthani? which is, being interpreted, My God, My God, Why hast Thou forsaken Me?" (Mark 15:34).

According to the 35th and 36th verses, no one really *knows* what He said. "And some of them that stood by, when they heard it, said, Behold, He calleth Elias. And one ran and filled a sponge full of vinegar, and put it on a reed, and gave Him to drink, saying, Let alone; let us see whether Elias will come to take Him down," (Mark 15:35-36).

Invoke A Blessing On Yourself.

Another example is found in The Book of John. "He groaned in the Spirit, and was troubled," (John 11:33). Then, He went to *raise* Lazarus from the dead. "Jesus therefore again groaning in Himself cometh to the grave," (John 11:38). If you do a word study, or if you are Spirit-filled, you will understand that Jesus was praying in tongues or praying in The Spirit.

His groaning was the same as praying in The Spirit. "...the Spirit itself maketh intercession for us with groanings which cannot be uttered," (Romans 8:26).

What Do These 3 Examples Mean?

If you *casually* read through these verses, you may miss an important revelation. These very verses *prove* Jesus prayed in The Spirit...*in tongues*. I do not believe this theory contradicts The Word of God, it only *strengthens* it.

That teaching alone is an entirely *different* book...

If you do not believe in speaking in tongues, then I am sorry that you do not. I simply ask that you put these examples on 'the shelf' and *stay* with me through the *end* of this book. If at that time you still do not agree, then you are free to believe *anything* you want.

Invoke A Blessing On Yourself.

However, if you are a *learner*, you will research and pray; and if you are *willing* to receive the revelation, The Holy Spirit will help you.

The Holy Spirit will send you mentors. "And He gave some, apostles; and some, prophets; and some, evangelists; and some, pastors and teachers; For the perfecting of the saints, for the work of the ministry, for the edifying of the body of Christ," (Ephesians 4:11-12).

Invoke A Blessing On Yourself.

I Will Praise Thee; For I Am Fearfully And Wonderfully Made: Marvelous Are Thy Works; And That My Soul Knoweth Right Well.

—Psalm 139:14

Invoke A Blessing On Yourself.

2

Did You Know The World Needs You?

You have value.

Our world requires new *ideas*, new *leaders*, new *inventors* and new *ways* of doing things more efficiently. In the book, *1,001 Wisdom Keys of Dr. Mike Murdock*, the 5th Wisdom Key reads, "Your Rewards In Life Are Determined By The Kinds of Problems You Are Willing To Solve For Others."

If you can provide a great product or service to solve someone's problem you will *greatly* succeed. As you probably already know, you cannot get anything of great value for *nothing*.

Invoke A Blessing On Yourself.

> Your Rewards In Life Are Determined By The Kinds of Problems You Are Willing To Solve For Others.
>
> -Dr. Mike Murdock

You need to make your dreams happen for *yourself*.

If you are waiting for someone to show up just to motivate you and get you started, you may have to wait for a long time.

What if no one shows up?

Write down your goals and vision.

Pray over them *daily*.

Focus your *thinking* on your dream.

Work on a *plan* of achievement toward it.

> Among The Secrets of The Super Rich, Perseverance Is More Important Than Intelligence.
>
> -Unknown

Do not give up unless giving up will get you the results you want!

Many years ago, a great warrior was *determined* to win a war against a formidable enemy. He was *resolute* in making sure he succeeded against his adversary. He was

Invoke A Blessing On Yourself.

also aware that this powerful foe's army had greatly *outnumbered* his forces.

He instructed his soldiers to get on boats and sail to the enemy's country. After they had unloaded all their equipment, and every soldier had disembarked on enemy territory, he ordered his men to *burn* the ships.

Before the battle even started, he told his soldiers, "Look! Do you see the boats going up in smoke? We will not leave these shores alive unless we win; so we now have no choice, but to win. We win or we perish."

They won.

Many of Life's Failures Are Because People Did Not Realize How Close They Came To Success Before They Gave Up. Never Give Up Unless Giving Up Will Get You What You Want.

-Yuri I. Tereshchenko

"Now to Him Who, by (in consequence of) the [action of His] power that is at work within us, is able to [carry out His purpose and] do superabundantly, far over and above all that we [dare] ask or think [infinitely beyond our highest prayers, desires, thoughts, hopes, or dreams]," (Ephesians 3:20 AMP).

Invoke A Blessing On Yourself.

If you set your mind to win, you will *win*; but you have to be militant about it and use wisdom. Each person is at a different *learning* and *faith* level. When you read a book for the first time, you absorb *some* knowledge. When you read the same book the second time, you read it as a *different* person.

When you gain new knowledge and information, you receive what you are reading and hearing on a completely different *frequency*, because you have since developed a different point of *view*. It will seem as if you have never heard that information before, like you are wearing a new or better pair of eye glasses.

By doing so, you will...*invoke a blessing on yourself.*

Invoke A Blessing On Yourself.

3

Where Did This All Begin?

You are God's greatest creation...*His greatest idea.*

"And God said, Let us make man in Our image, after our likeness: and let them have dominion over the fish of the sea, and over the fowl of the air, and over the cattle, and over all the earth, and over every creeping thing that creepeth upon the earth," (Genesis 1:26).

"Yet You have made him but a little lower than God [or heavenly beings], and You have crowned him with glory and honor," (Psalm 8:5 AMP).

Have you thought about the fact that our Father God wanted to create someone that was a little lower than *Himself*, in His image and in His likeness? He created everything by *speaking* it into existence.

Invoke A Blessing On Yourself.

You Shall Have Whatsoever You Say!

-Mark 11:23

Invoke A Blessing On Yourself.

Be careful what you say, because as your faith *increases*, your words will have *more* power. Your faith will *create* an uncommon Future for you.

Remember to *say* what He *said*.

> I have set before you life and death, blessing and cursing: therefore choose life, that both thou and thy seed may live.
>
> Deuteronomy 30:19

I heard a pastor talking about an experience he had while snorkeling. Somehow, he got *separated* from the group he was swimming with. Then he saw a school of sharks coming his way.

He remembered that he had *authority* over the sharks and over *all* the things in the earth. (See Genesis 1:26). So, he *commanded* the sharks to *look*, but not to taste; because he is on a *higher* level of the food chain.

Let me add a few more examples here.

When you say: "I am *dying* to tell you," or "that tickled me to *death*," and other death-talk, like "that just *kills* me," or "that just *breaks* my heart," remember Proverbs 18:21. "Death and life are in the power of the tongue: and they that love it shall eat the fruit thereof."

Say what God says. Speak life, do not speak death.

Invoke A Blessing On Yourself.

Never say, "I am dying to do this or I am dying to do that." If you must say such a crazy thing, replace death with *life*.

Speak what you want, not what you do not want.

Become Attentive To What You Say.

Record yourself throughout the day and then listen to the words you *habitually* speak. Ask people around you if they think you are positive or negative. If you do not have someone to ask, that should be a clue!

Do not give so much credit to the devil. He will take the credit even when it is not due him. The devil is all roar and no *bite*, unless you give *in* to him. "Be sober, be vigilant; because your adversary the devil, as a roaring lion, walketh about, seeking whom he may devour," (1 Peter 5:8). "Submit yourselves therefore to God. Resist the devil, and he will flee from you," (James 4:7).

Create a *picture* in your Mind by what you *say*.

If you do not feel good, do not speak that over yourself. Instead, declare, "I am getting better."

Command your body.

Your spirit is in charge of your body. Do not give the devil charge over your body by speaking *wrong* words. You may be thinking that speaking the opposite of what you are feeling is a lie.

Invoke A Blessing On Yourself.

No! Not really.

If you feel bad, do not say *how* you feel, because you will feel what you say. Instead, say what you *want* to feel. When you say, "I am getting better," your body *hears* that message and *responds* to your command. *Tell* your body what you *want* to feel.

Your Body Is Not You.

You are a *spirit*.

You have a soul and you *live* in a body. Your body is a *suit*. Your body is a *vehicle*. You tell your body *what* to do and *how* to do it. You tell your body *where* to go, *when* to go, and so on. What kind of commands are you giving your body?

We will cover this in depth in the chapters ahead.

There is a lot of scientific evidence that proves that your body and every single thing that was created, like the trees, the ocean, even the mountains; were all made of the same matter. It was *proven* by Einstein and Edison that the brain can send or receive *vibrational* frequency. Every single thing on earth *emits* a different frequency. Everything is composed of the same molecules and energy. There are different materials, colors, shapes and sizes because of differences in *frequency*.

Invoke A Blessing On Yourself.

Your Body Is A Temple:
Are You Taking Care of Your Temple?

Our body *contains* DNA.

Our DNA *stores* data.

Our DNA is a communication mechanism which receives, interprets and processes that data.

There is evidence of a whole new discipline of medicine in which DNA can be influenced and reprogrammed by words and frequencies *without* cutting out and replacing single genes.

Since our DNA is capable of receiving new data and processing it, you have an option to *manipulate* the genetic code in your favor. You can modulate certain frequency patterns with your words. In response, your DNA converts those words into laser-like rays which influence DNA frequency and consequently the genetic information itself.

Everything Around You Has Ears.

Everything around you *hears* what you say.

When you say, "Father God, I come to you in The Strong Name of Jesus Christ of Nazareth," all ears *perk* up. As you continue, "I thank You that I am healed. Cancer is just a name. Diabetes is just a name. The Bible says in

Invoke A Blessing On Yourself.

Philippians 2:10, "that at The Name of Jesus every knee should bow, of things in heaven, and things in earth, and things under the earth," so I curse that cancer and I command it to dry up at the roots. I command it to dissipate and to dry up in The Mighty Name of Jesus Christ of Nazareth."

Now, as you are full of faith and conviction, do not dare say, "I am battling cancer," or whatever it is you think you are contending with.

The Prayer For Healing Is Simply Agreeing With What Jesus Already Did For Us On The Cross.

The above prayer is a *done* deal. You simply confirmed and *agreed* with all of what He did. Jesus *fought* the whole battle for you at The Cross. "And having spoiled principalities and powers, He made a shew of them openly, triumphing over them in it," (Colossians 2:10).

Every time you are questioned about your situation or feel any doubt, just declare, "I thank The Father that I am healed." You may not have the manifestation of your healing, but you have faith; so use it to your *advantage*.

This biblically and scientifically explains why affirmations, positive words (in some cases people use

Invoke A Blessing On Yourself.

hypnosis) and the like can have such *strong* effects on humans and their bodies. It is entirely normal and natural for our DNA to *react* to words. It has been known for ages that our body is *programmable* by language, words and thought.

The problem with many Christian believers is *ignorance* and a lack of understanding of The Word of God. "My people are destroyed for lack of knowledge..." (Hosea 4:6). The Bible *clearly* says: "You can have whatsoever you say..." (See Mark 11:23.)

The concept of speaking things into existence is so powerful, it can even be done *remotely*. You can speak healing over the phone and also via television. You can also speak a blessing to someone *thousands* of miles away, even *without* the assistance of electronic or digital media, and your faith will *impact* the intended destination.

Due to copyright laws, I will not be adding extensive amounts of research material to this book. If you are interested in getting more information, or if you are skeptical, there are a lot of books and articles available that you can study on this topic.

As you speak things into existence, it helps to understand the *frequency* that will attract *quicker* results. That is one of the reasons you are reading this book...*to gain knowledge*. "And God blessed them, and God said unto them, Be fruitful, and multiply, and replenish the

Invoke A Blessing On Yourself.

earth, and subdue it: and have dominion over the fish of the sea, and over the fowl of the air, and over every living thing that moveth upon the earth," (Genesis 1:28).

Invoke A Blessing On Yourself.

The Blessing of The LORD, It Maketh Rich, And He Addeth No Sorrow With It.

-Proverbs 10:22

Invoke A Blessing On Yourself.

4

God Wants You To Be Blessed

Your Creator created you to *live* The Blessed Life.

God, our Father, wants us to grow, multiply, succeed, prosper and be in good health.

So, what do you have to do?

Invoke a blessing on yourself, by saying what God is saying about you. You can have whatsoever you say.

"For verily I say unto you, That whosoever shall say unto this mountain, Be thou removed, and be thou cast into the sea; and shall not doubt in his heart, but shall believe that those things which he saith shall come to pass; he shall have whatsoever he saith," (Mark 11:23).

Invoke A Blessing On Yourself.

You Can Have Whatever You Desire.

You can have the desires of your heart as long as they are *biblically* based. "Delight thyself also in the Lord; and He shall give thee the desires of thine heart. Commit thy way unto the Lord; trust also in Him; and He shall bring it to pass," (Psalm 37:4-5).

If you desire your friend's wife, this book is not for you. If you desire something that is going to hurt you or others, this book is not for you.

As you begin to apply the principles in this book, you will become so *blessed* you will be in a position to bless *others*. Instead of saying that you have to work hard for your money say, "Money comes to me easily, frequently and consistently."

When we developed the desire to make more money, I got a revelation: Tithe on what you want to make, on what you want to keep, and on what you want to protect...*not on what you currently make.*

When I was earning $2,500 a month we tithed $300 because we believed that God would raise us to make $3000 a month. Once we were blessed to make that much, we decided to tithe *more*.

Anything you give above your Tithe is a Seed...*and it was*. It was a Seed of faith for *increase*. In addition, we

Invoke A Blessing On Yourself.

sowed *additional* Seed for various church projects as The Lord would lead us.

When I owned my own *Lawn Care and Snow Removal Business* in Nebraska, we would tithe on *every* single dollar that the business brought in. It was tough because normally, if you have a $10,000 project, $5,000 of that money would go to materials and $3,000 may go to pay the employees.

Out of that $2,000 was my *personal* pay to keep. We would tithe on the *entire* $10,000, so $1,000 would go to our church. As a result God blessed us *wonderfully*.

We had set aside working with this principle for awhile, but The Holy Spirit has began to stir us again. We have started to tithe on more than I make, because we want the windows of Heaven to be *opened* over us.

This is an act of faith for us. It worked in the past, so we keep doing it. You have to *build* your faith like a *muscle*. Feed your faith with The Word of God.

Stretch yourself...*grow and mature*. You will derive great pleasure as you see yourself grow.

Now Faith Is The Substance of Things Hoped For And The Evidence of Things Not Seen.

-Hebrews 11:1

Invoke A Blessing On Yourself.

You will need to believe for a pair of socks or a tie before you will have the faith for something bigger, like a car or a house. In this book, I share some personal life and death testimonies. I want to preface my testimony by stating that for about four years I was self employed, so we did not have a very good health insurance plan.

Furthermore, when we had the choice to pray and believe, or drop several thousand dollars at the doctor's office that we were not in a position to spend at the time, we chose to live by faith.

Radical faith did not just happen automatically, nor did anything of value appear in our lives without a cause. We are thankful to God for our growth in this process.

Grow your faith and…*invoke a blessing on yourself.*

Invoke A Blessing On Yourself.

5

How Committed Are You To Changing Things In Your Life?

Sin is a *destroyer*.

Look carefully at what happened to Cain. Here is the Contemporary English Version. "The LORD said to Cain: What's wrong with you? Why do you have such an angry look on your face? If you had done the right thing, you would be smiling. But you did the wrong thing, and now sin is waiting to attack you like a lion. Sin wants to destroy you, but don't let it!" (Genesis 4:6-7 CEV).

Cain wanted to present the sacrifice his *way* and on his own *terms*. Most people want to grow and change, but

Invoke A Blessing On Yourself.

You Are One Decision Away From Radical Change

– Dr. Mike Murdock

Invoke A Blessing On Yourself.

want to do it *their* way. After a while they realize that if they keep doing the same thing they will keep getting the same results, over and over.

You must become conscious of *what* you need to change and *where* you need to grow. Be prepared to discern, accept and understand what is required of you to make the necessary changes. Look for the environment that makes you learn and change; and become *actively* involved in it.

Don't Wish Things Were Easier, Wish You Were Better.
-Jim Rohn

Recently, I was thinking about a certain individual.

I thought how much more *enjoyable* his life would be if he would make a *few* changes. At that very moment The Spirit of The Lord reminded me that if I would make small improvements in my *own* life, it would be much easier and more enjoyable. *Wow, how wonderful it is to have The Precious Holy Spirit!*

I took on a *new* challenge.

I made a decision to become *better*.

Invoke A Blessing On Yourself.

So, Where Do I Start...?

I am reminded of a quote by Jim Rohn, "Don't wish things were easier, wish you were better."

You may not be sure how to go about making changes and setting goals for your self improvement. We rarely ask one another, "What are my negative points?" or "What would you say I need to improve?"

The reason we avoid such interrogation is because it is hard to *admit* our own weaknesses. It is difficult to admit that we *need* to change. However, the only way to become more *secure* as a person is to recognize and admit your weaknesses.

The Significant Problems We Face Cannot Be Solved At The Same Level of Thinking We Were At When We Created Them.

- Albert Einstein

The best path to accomplishing change is with the help of another...*someone who really cares about you.*

This person will not be a perfect friend, but because they love you and because they only want the best for you, they are the most *qualified* to tell you about yourself.

Invoke A Blessing On Yourself.

Albert Einstein said, "The significant problems we face cannot be solved at the same level of thinking we were at when we created them."

Depending on what you long to accomplish, this type of change may take days, months, years, or maybe a lifetime. The main issue is whether you want to become a better person and *work* at it; or if you are just hoping that with time you will slowly *evolve*.

Make no mistake; time is not the main ingredient for any major change you want to accomplish. There are numerous broke and miserable people who are advanced in years; yet there are also many wealthy and successful individuals who made significant achievements at an early age.

In the following chapters you will read more about having a *mentor* and listening to the *right* voice.

Which One of These Traps Is Keeping You From Achieving Your Goals?

1. *Wrong Focus.*
2. *Wrong Thoughts And Words.* Thoughts and words can deter you from your goals. Thoughts and words are *magnifiers* of your experiences.
3. *Forgetting Your True Goal.* You may have become so involved with your present circumstances that

Invoke A Blessing On Yourself.

you forgot the bigger picture...*your life purpose.* It is *easy* to lose sight of your goals if you become preoccupied with your frustration and disappointment.

4. *Your Upbringing.* Maybe you were raised in an environment where every time your father looked at the newspaper, he announced that the stock market was down; therefore the economy was down, business was down, and everything was stacked *against* your family. As you *internalize* this kind of thinking, you will *drift* from your goals and start to feel sorry for yourself. Are you using your Past as an *excuse* that your Future cannot get any better?

If you have fallen into any of these traps, take some time to refocus, pray and get back on course.

How Do You Rate On Your Ability To Accept And Embrace Change?

Times are *changing*.

We need to keep up with the changes in our environment and society. Jobs and businesses that existed and thrived five years ago, no longer exist. Payphones and video rental stores are not as popular as they used to be. Residential landline phone service is becoming *obsolete*. People are using cell phones and the internet more and more. Some jobs have been *eliminated*

Invoke A Blessing On Yourself.

or are *disappearing* because of computerization. The Information Age is *revolutionizing* the way we live and work.

If you were raised in a different country than where you now live, you will have to deal with cultural differences. Every culture has its own *unique* attributes.

Be patient, flexible and listen to The Voice of The Holy Spirit. Study, learn, prepare and be sure to constantly...*invoke a blessing on yourself.*

Invoke A Blessing On Yourself.

Most People Plan Their Vacations With Better Care Than They Plan Their Lives. Perhaps That Is Because Escape Is Easier Than Change.

-Jim Rohn

Invoke A Blessing On Yourself.

6

How About A Friend...For A Change?

> You Can't Invoke Progress In Your Life Without Change And Those Who Cannot Change Their Minds Cannot Change Anything.
>
> – Yuri I. Tereshchenko

Change requires motivation.

Obesity is a prevalent problem in The United States of America today. Many people desire to *lose* weight. Trying to lose weight by yourself is a difficult accomplishment, especially if you have no motivation. Of

Invoke A Blessing On Yourself.

the many success stories about weight loss that we hear, the individuals usually give credit to someone or something that motivated them. If your goal is to change your *inner* self emotionally, it is a much more complicated feat than *physically* losing weight.

That is why it is important to have someone by your side. If you cannot trust anyone to help you, you may have to reconsider if this is for you. "Two are better than one; because they have a good reward for their labour. For if they fall, the one will lift up his fellow: but woe to him that is alone when he falleth; for he hath not another to help him up," (Ecclesiastes 4:9-10).

> An Uncommon Future Will Require Uncommon Preparation.
>
> -Dr. Mike Murdock

The first sign of the *inferiority* complex is the inability to trust *anyone*. It is true that you cannot trust all people or even most; however, you must have *someone* you can trust, at least *one* person, to begin with.

No one promised this would be *easy*.

You do not need things to be easier; but, you have to be *realistic*. Focus on becoming *better*. Focus on *growth*.

If you are not growing, you are *dying*.

Invoke A Blessing On Yourself.

If you are not learning, you are not growing.
If you are not seeking, you are not learning.
Our nature craves growth and learning.
When you are driving a car, you will not see as far as ten or twenty cities ahead of you; but you may see *one* mile in front of you, and that is *enough*.
You accomplish things in life one *mile* at a time.
Where will you start? Anything of value and greatness was accomplished by a plan. You must have a plan in place. Set the goals you want to accomplish. You cannot aim at a target you have not identified.
If you *fail* to plan you *plan* to fail.

Document Your Thoughts And Experiences Daily In A Journal.

1. Put together a list of weaknesses, things you want to change about yourself, and the areas where you want to grow.

2. Create a list of things you are working on, so you know the areas you may experience struggle.

Pray over your list. Let The Holy Spirit talk to you and direct you on the best *strategy* for accomplishing your goals.

All through the day, and *every* day, write in your journal. Write down your accomplishments. Document

Invoke A Blessing On Yourself.

the areas where you have improved and the areas where you still need further development.

This will create a live record of your progress.

Progress is a *must*.

Progress is what fuels excitement.

Progress will birth *daily* purpose.

As you document your progress, you will notice discouragement, stress and depression *leaving*. Writing down your feelings will help you. As you journal, you will *unload* negativity.

The Holy Spirit will speak to your spirit.

Why do you have to write all of this down? Your close friends may not *always* be available or in the mood to sit and listen to you unload your emotional baggage, but your journal *is* there for you anytime.

Write everything that comes to your Mind.

See Yourself Having What You Want.

Once your Mind is clear, think on things that you want to have and see yourself having them.

Believe that you *have* them.

Remember, The Bible says in Mark 11:24, "Therefore I say unto you, What things soever ye desire, when ye pray, believe that ye receive them, and ye shall have them."

Invoke A Blessing On Yourself.

You may have read and heard this scripture numerous times. Unfortunately, there are only a few people that can explain it until it is *clearly* understood.

The 3 Step Formula To Receiving What You Want.

1. The first step of the formula is to *ask*. If you do not ask, no one can help you. The Bible teaches us in James 4:2, "You have not, because you ask not."
2. The second step of the formula is to *believe*. Use your faith. "Without faith it is impossible to please God…" (Hebrews 11:6).
3. The third part of the formula is to *receive*. This is a *critical* step. Many believers who have mastered Step 1 and 2 have aborted the process by failing with Step 3.

How To Be A Great Receiver.

There are many aspects to being a great receiver. I want to review a couple of them.

You have to be grateful for what you *have* and what you *get*. Take care of that house or car that you currently possess. Be proud of it. When someone does something good for you, or gives you a gift, be *thankful*.

Be *really* thankful. Learn to be *more* thankful. This is an area I am really working on right now in my *own*

Invoke A Blessing On Yourself.

life. It is so easy to be indifferent and unthankful. Ingratitude *kills* your harvests. Ingratitude is like a cancer that will kill the blessings in your life.

It is a pleasure to be around a *thankful* person.

Gifts Reveal The Character of Those Who Receive Them.

-Dr. Mike Murdock

---

1 Chronicles 16:34 instructs us, "O give thanks unto the LORD; for He is good; for His mercy endureth for ever."

Always keep a spirit of thankfulness, because thankfulness *qualifies* you for more of what you want and need. Thankfulness alone will bring you joy; and because you are thankful, new harvests will bring you more joy.

If you can change anything, embrace The Law of Thankfulness. This Law will help you…*invoke a blessing on yourself.*

Invoke A Blessing On Yourself.

7

Are You Abiding By The Law?

The entire universe runs by Laws.

There are Laws in The Universe that were set by God, that do not change. The Law of Gravity works whether you believe it or not. If you, as a skeptic, stepped off the roof of a building, you will quickly *recognize* and *experience* The Law of Gravity. The only difference is, if it is a one story building, you will live to share your 'testimony.' If the building is two or more stories, we will see you in heaven...*hopefully*.

Learn The Laws of The Universe. Ignorance is not an excuse. Living in ignorance does not *exempt* you from experiencing the effects of The Laws of the universe.

Invoke A Blessing On Yourself.

For Every Success That You Had, There Was A Law That You Honored; For Every Failure That You Had, There Was A Law That You Broke.

- Dr. Mike Murdock

Invoke A Blessing On Yourself.

If you are happy with your present success, but still have a desire to learn more, then you are a *great* student. If you are sitting there saying, "Oh! I already know all this," that kind of attitude is not going to get you very far. It will *abort* all future discoveries.

What Are You Teaching Your Children...By Your Daily Actions?

Let me share with you a story I heard from a great man of God. It is the story of a father and his son. When the son was just a boy, his father parked illegally. When the son noticed that his father was not obeying the traffic rules, he asked his father, "Why did you park where we were not supposed to?"

The father *arrogantly* replied, "We will not be here for a long time. It does not really matter where I park."

Some years later, the father received a phone call about his son. His son had been involved in a tragic accident because he had *illegally* overtaken a car on the highway. The father, through his actions, had told his son that breaking rules was acceptable.

Now, his son lay *dead*.

You will lead by example...good or bad.

Someone is *always* watching.

Invoke A Blessing On Yourself.

My dad *constantly* talked to us about traffic rules, "What good is it if you have the right of way, but ruin your automobile, crack your skull or get crippled for the rest of your life?" I will never forget that statement because he kept repeating it over and over.

Become A Person of High Integrity.

I went to an auto parts store with my six year old son. While I was ordering parts for my truck, my son kept himself busy by playing with some tools. After we returned home, my son came up to me with tears in his eyes. "Daddy I am sorry. I put this tool in my pocket, and I forgot to leave it at the store."

I consoled him and thanked him for his honesty in telling me what he had done. I assured him I would drop it off at the store the following day. That tool sat on the front seat of my car for *several* days. It seemed as if I was too busy to return it to the store.

I heard this story of the father and his son at a Sunday morning service. That afternoon, my son and I made the trip to the auto parts store to *return* the tool.

It did not matter that it was worth less than $1. We choose to teach our children honesty and integrity, among other things.

Invoke A Blessing On Yourself.

If I had trivialized that act, what would I have taught my six year old?

What could possibly happen to him later in life if he grew up knowing that if his father could get away with something, he could too?

> Every Law Contains A Different Reward.
>
> -Dr. Mike Murdock

Be diligent in honesty, integrity and honor.

The jails are full of people that ignored laws.

Make sure you develop the *right* attitude toward laws. It is said that when a criminal commits a crime for the first time, they *despise* what they did. When they commit a crime for the second and third times, they *lose* the feeling of guilt. After a while it becomes a *normal* way of life.

After committing many crimes, it becomes a *passion* for them. They become *attached* and *addicted* to the criminal lifestyle. The life of holiness may work in a similar way. After you have sacrificed and worked so hard to live a holy life, it becomes your passion to live *pure*. "Flee also youthful lusts: but follow righteousness, faith, charity, peace, with them that call on the Lord out of a pure heart," (2 Timothy 2:22).

Invoke A Blessing On Yourself.

In Matthew 16:19, we find the following words, "And I will give unto thee the keys of the kingdom of heaven: and whatsoever thou shalt bind on earth shall be bound in heaven: and whatsoever thou shalt loose on earth shall be loosed in heaven."

You have the power and authority to act on the earth as a *representative* of The Almighty. Use that authority given to you to *invoke a blessing on yourself*...so you can in turn change the world and bless others.

Invoke A Blessing On Yourself.

8

Are You Ready For Your Miracle Experience?

Attitude overrides facts.

Your attitude is far *superior* to beliefs. In the end, for the most part, beliefs are simply people's opinions. In the 19th century, there was a popular belief that nothing heavier than air could fly, but now we know there is a superior law to The Law of Gravity, *The Law of Lift*.

Whatever you *repeatedly* tell yourself, whether it is the truth or a lie, you will eventually *believe* as if it were a fact. If you keep telling yourself a *lie*, eventually you will believe it to be *truth*.

I knew a lady who used to believe she was ugly.

Invoke A Blessing On Yourself.

Let Others Lead Average Lives, But Not You; Lead A Supernatural Life.

-Yuri I. Tereshchenko

Invoke A Blessing On Yourself.

Her mother convinced her of this, so she would not be attracted to boys and fall into sin, so she looked *plain*. Once she was married, she was able to express her outward beauty *freely* and became one of the *most* beautiful young ladies that I know.

You *become* what you think about most of the time.

You *have* what you think about most of the time.

Consider the following scripture, "Whatsoever things are true, whatsoever things are honest, whatsoever things are just, whatsoever things are pure, whatsoever things are lovely, whatsoever things are of good report; if there be any virtue, and if there be any praise, think on these things," (Philippians 4:8).

Reverend Kenneth E. Hagin came into the world with a deformed heart and an incurable blood disease. At the time of his birth that was a fact, however he was healed by The Blood of Jesus.

His attitude *changed* the facts in his life.

Your Attitude Will Change The Facts In Your Life.

One day, while I was at work, our son slipped on the wood floor and hit his head on the marble slab at the bottom of our fireplace. He was bleeding profusely. It appeared he needed stitches, so my wife had to respond

Invoke A Blessing On Yourself.

quickly. We prayed for *quick* healing because we did not want to *have* to take him to the hospital.

She commanded the bleeding to stop in The Name of Jesus. *It stopped immediately.*

One evening, my wife and I were moving some furniture into our apartment. It was dark and we had to stop to take a break. My wife unknowingly stepped on an ant hill. Ten minutes later, she felt very itchy. Her face became swollen and her whole body was covered with red rash-like spots. Several minutes later, she started losing consciousness. She was having difficulty breathing.

Within a few minutes, her condition became very serious. We called on The Name of The Lord for *immediate* healing. We pleaded The Blood of Jesus over her. It looked like her condition kept getting worse, so I offered to take her to the hospital.

"Only Jesus Can Save Me Now...!"

She thought for a moment and then responded, with a weak voice, "There will be no time to get to the hospital, because my condition is getting worse by the minute. Only Jesus can save me now."

A minute or so later, she yelled, "Jesus," then passed out. Later, she regained consciousness. She told

Invoke A Blessing On Yourself.

me she was feeling a little better and that she would be fine. By morning she was *completely* healed.

The facts are, her body could have shut down and she could have died. But, our attitude was, The Power of God is stronger than the poison of hundreds of ants biting and *infecting* her body.

The Miracles You Experience Will Cause Your Faith To Grow.

When my son was only five, he jumped off the couch and severely injured his wrist. His hand was blue. You could not even touch his hand. Moving it slightly caused him enormous amounts of pain.

Again, we believed for supernatural healing.

It took three very long weeks for him to *completely* recover, but our faith grew. Now, he knows that Jesus *can* and *will* heal him. Our daughter had witnessed how much pain her brother had been in and was now healed, so her faith *grew* as well.

We prayed *daily* to The Father, in The Name of Jesus, for his *complete* healing. Our trust was not in a pill, but, under the guidance of The Holy Spirit, in The Power of The All Powerful, Almighty God.

Invoke A Blessing On Yourself.

You will get what you *think* you deserve...*good or bad*. If you will allow and tolerate being mistreated in any way, you will get what you expect.

Our Father wants us to *have* good things.
Our Father wants us to *prosper*.
Our Father wants us to be *blessed*.

My Wisdom Tooth Miracle

During the writing of this book, I experienced pain in one of my teeth. It may have been a wisdom tooth. I decided to pray for Divine direction on what to do next.

As I was praying, The Holy Spirit prompted me to put that problem on my prayer list. Every morning, I go through my list. I call on The Father in The Mighty Name of Jesus of Nazareth. I *thank* Him for everything He does. As I thank Him, my body *responds* to what I am saying.

I began to thank Him for *healing* my tooth. Every morning I said, "Father, thank You for healing my tooth. I thank You that the tooth is restored and functioning perfectly as it should."

Notice I did not say, "Father if it is Your will."

I did not say, "Please take the pain away."

I was not praying the problem. I was praying the solution...*the desired result*. Every time I felt pain, I thanked The Father. This went on throughout the day. It

Invoke A Blessing On Yourself.

took a couple of days, but the pain *eventually* went away. A couple of weeks later, the tooth was no longer sensitive. Within a few weeks, I started using that side of my mouth to chew my food.

Praise God for He can renew and restore our teeth and anything else we need…even without the help of dentists or doctors.

Speak it.
Believe it.
Receive it.
Name it.
Claim it.

Whatever Goal Your Mind Can Conceive And Believe It Can Achieve. You Can Invoke Any Conceivable Blessing

-Yuri I. Tereshchenko

Consider these words from Ecclesiastes 11:4, in The Message Bible, "Don't sit there watching the wind. Do your own work. Don't stare at the clouds. Get on with your life."

Learn to *manage* every moment and you will get the best *return* on your time investments. Spend time daily in learning to become a *better* person. You will

Invoke A Blessing On Yourself.

never meet an unsuccessful person who is particular about his time. Unsuccessful people are not conscious of their time or the proper use of it.

You can move a mountain...one *pebble* at a time.

How much are you *willing* to change? Are you willing to discard wrong facts, ideas and opinions? Are you willing to trust God, step out and use your faith; instead of following the crowd and doing what is comfortable and convenient?

Are you willing to change...to *invoke a blessing on yourself?*

Invoke A Blessing On Yourself.

9

Are You Ready To Predict Your Future?

Your vision is your *picture* of the Future.

When you look at an acorn what do you see? I hope your answer is not "food for squirrels." When you see an acorn, do you see an oak tree, a forest, lumber or houses? In this chapter, I will cover the depth of vision.

You must set daily, weekly, monthly, yearly and lifetime goals. Without goals, it will be *impossible* for you to succeed. Write your goals down so you can visualize them *every* day.

Pray over your goals *every* day.

Invoke A Blessing On Yourself.

Your Future Will Not Let You Enter Without A Change

-Dr. Mike Murdock

Invoke A Blessing On Yourself.

You cannot hit a target you cannot see. You cannot do a thing unless you *imagine* it, *visualize* it and *believe* you can do it.

There are some great books you can get on goal-setting. Some of the best ones I have read have been written by Dr. Mike Murdock.

> You Can't Invoke A Blessing Unless You Imagine It, Visualize It And Believe You Can Do It Or Have It.
> -Yuri I. Tereshchenko

There are three words that will *hinder* your progress in life. They may be the three most *dangerous* words you could ever say.

Those words are, "I know that."

When you say, "I know that," you command your brain to shut down because any forthcoming information has no importance. You have also told the person speaking to you that you are not interested in hearing what they have to say.

It is true, you may already know what is being said, but sometimes it helps to be reminded. You may learn a *new* variation and revelation of what you *already* know.

Invoke A Blessing On Yourself.

I want to alert you to an interesting fact about Methuselah. Methuselah was the *oldest* person in The Bible. He lived the *longest*. "And all the days of Methuselah were nine hundred sixty and nine years: and he died," (Genesis 5:27).

Some people are so slow in getting things done that I cannot help but think of them as Methuselah. It seems they would need many years to get anything accomplished.

Will you leave a legacy when you die?

Will you be the example of what to do or the example of what not to do?

Become *somebody*, do not be just anybody; because you are a child of The Almighty God.

Expect Good Things To Happen In Your Life.

When you pray, be *grateful* to The Father for everything you have already received. Name what you need and believe you have already received it...*and you will receive it*.

If you have already lived 30, 40, 50, or more, years on this earth, and you are still broke, you are doing something *wrong*. Think on these words from The Book of Proverbs. "A good man leaveth an inheritance to his children's children," (Proverbs 13:22).

Invoke A Blessing On Yourself.

>Become *willing* to learn.
>*Write* down your goals.
>Become a *lifelong* learner.
>Develop the *vision* for your life.
>Don't go around saying: "I know that."

Learn from *every* moment, situation and opportunity; otherwise you will never develop a legacy for your life.

I would like to finish this chapter with a story about Napoleon Hill's son. He was born *without* ears. According to the doctors, he was destined to be dumb and a mute. Mr. Hill, shockingly, *refused* to accept that prognosis.

Because of his faith and perseverance, Mr. Hill discovered that sound could be *transferred* through a bone in his head. His son could listen to music by putting his teeth on a musical instrument.

Later, when the child grew up, he got a job with a company that manufactured hearing aids. Having read such an amazing story, I hope you will *never* give up.

Imagine.
See your Future...*and decide to live there.*

Invoke A Blessing On Yourself.

Your Thoughts Birth Ideas, Your Ideas Birth Your Future Accomplishments And Your Success.
    -Yuri I. Tereshchenko

Invoke A Blessing On Yourself.

10

You Too Can Create Your Own Future

You decide your own Future.

If you want to *predict* your Future, *create* it.

You get what you *think* about most of the time.

If you want a nice watch, put up a picture of the watch that you want. Be *flexible*. Do not attach a time frame to when you will receive it, because you may be disappointed. Be open-minded about how you will receive it.

Someone could *give* you that watch.

Another may give you the *money* for that watch.

You could find such a great *deal* on that particular watch that you choose to buy it.

Invoke A Blessing On Yourself.

If you are happy and excited about the watch, you will get it; but if you have doubts and a lack of faith for it, you are *not* likely to receive it.

If you picture yourself happy with that watch, that is what is going to *attract* the watch into your life.

What To Do...When You Have No Faith.

What do you do when you just do not have enough faith, but have plenty of doubt about getting that watch?

The reason you have doubt could be because you are trying to figure out who would give you the *watch*, who would give you the *money* for the watch, or how you were going to *pay* for that $2,000 watch...that you really cannot afford right now. You will never get that watch unless you *change* your thinking.

Do not spend your time thinking about *how* to get it. Spend your time thinking about how you are going to *enjoy* the watch. Think about how that watch is going to compliment your outfit. Think of the ways you will enjoy *your* $2,000 watch.

The reason most people are unable to *predict* or *create* their Future is because they look at their situation through a *small* screen.

Invoke A Blessing On Yourself.

Are You Looking At Your Life Through The 'Small' Screen?

If you wanted to drive from New York to California, you would look at your GPS screen; which normally will not show you the whole road unless you change some settings. You *trust* that the GPS system will lead you to your destination, no matter how far it is.

Even though you cannot see the *whole* trip laid out in front of you, you already know that beyond the portion of the journey visible on the GPS screen, there are roads and instructions to get to those roads, so you will still be able to reach your destination via the *fastest* route or the *shortest* distance.

The Bible contains a guide to *what* and *how* we should be thinking. "Rejoice in the Lord always: and again I say, Rejoice. Let your moderation be known unto all men. The Lord is at hand.

"Be careful for nothing; but in everything by prayer and supplication with thanksgiving let your requests be made known unto God.

"And the peace of God, which passeth all understanding, shall keep your hearts and minds through Christ Jesus.

"Finally, brethren, whatsoever things are true, whatsoever things are honest, whatsoever things are just,

Invoke A Blessing On Yourself.

whatsoever things are pure, whatsoever things are lovely, whatsoever things are of good report; if there be any virtue, and if there be any praise, think on these things," (Philippians 4:4-8).

You Get What You Really Want.

If there is something you really, really want; *you will get it.* If there is something you really, really do not want, you will get that too.

You *get* what you think about *most* of the time. I will cover this even more in the chapter on Job.

Going back to the example about the watch, if you really, really want that watch, and you think about it most of the time, you will *eventually* get it, even though you are not really sure *how*.

Let me share with you a story of a person who really, really wanted a Mercedes Benz. He would talk about the kind of Mercedes he wanted. He *constantly* shared about *what* he would do and *where* he would go if he got that wonderful car.

At the time, he could not really afford one, but he chose to think about it *most* of the time.

He *knew* the principles I am writing about in this book, so he kept telling himself and others around him

Invoke A Blessing On Yourself.

that he would get the Mercedes that he really, really wanted, even though he did not know how.

He did not spend any time thinking about the *how*.

The Missing Briefcase.

One day, while he was walking down the street, he noticed an abandoned briefcase next to a building. He looked through it, found the owner's phone number, and then contacted him.

The man on the other line was so excited because all his *personal* documents were in the bag, which he thought he had *lost*. He was so thankful that this stranger had been nice enough to contact him.

A short time later, they met face to face.

The bag had not been locked, but the papers inside were still secure. The papers were so important to the owner that he wanted to *offer* the man that found the bag *reward* money. The man who found the bag responded that he was only trying to be a *good* citizen. He was not really expecting to get a reward for *returning* the bag.

The owner of the bag was so grateful, he *insisted* on giving the honest man a reward, so he wrote him a check for $50,000.

The man who had a desire for the Mercedes had no idea *how* he would get it, but he used his faith to call it in.

Invoke A Blessing On Yourself.

He did not sit there attempting to figure out how much the payments would be. With the reward money he was able to get what he had *believed* for.

> An Uncommon Dream Requires Uncommon Patience.
>
> -Dr. Mike Murdock

In Matthew 17:20, we read, "...for verily I say unto you, If ye have faith as a grain of mustard seed, ye shall say unto this mountain, Remove hence to yonder place; and it shall remove; and nothing shall be impossible unto you."

Invoke A Blessing On Yourself.

11

It's Not The How, It's When...!

Do not worry about the how, only *believe*.

If you desire a particular car, think about *driving* it.

Think about *who* you can bless and the type of people you will *attract* when you have this car.

Everyone around you will try to get you to figure out the how, but do not give in. Do not worry about the how, just *believe* and *know* that it will work out and happen.

The things that you want are *already* here, you just cannot see them with your physical eyes. When you look at your 3" radar screen or your GPS, it may seem like

Invoke A Blessing On Yourself.

The People Who Know Their God Shall Be Strong And Do Great Things.
—Daniel 11:32 TLB

Invoke A Blessing On Yourself.

there is no possible way you could get what you want, but your Future is bigger than the 3" screen you are looking at.

This is how I got the title for this great book: *Invoke a Blessing on Yourself.*

I never thought I would get the assignment to write such an important book for The Body of Christ. When I received the idea for this book, I knew I had to follow through with it. When you realize the *potential* of this principle, you will get *new* business ideas and inventions...*more than anything you could possibly imagine.*

Ideas Can Be Life-Changing. Sometimes All You Need Is To Invoke Just One More Great Idea.

-Yuri I. Tereshchenko

Do not be concerned about the *how*.

If you are driving while talking on a cell phone, or you are looking for a particular street, you may overlook a lot of details around you because of your given focus.

In life, you must focus on the *positive*...focus on the *finish line*...focus on the *Harvest*.

Trying to figure out *how* you will get there is not important. Just concentrate on the *present* moment.

The present moment will get you to the *end* result.

Invoke A Blessing On Yourself.

The present moment will *introduce* you to the how.

This Secret Will Change Your Life.

You can *have*, *be* or *do* anything that you want according to The Gospel of Mark. "For verily I say unto you, That whosoever shall say unto this mountain, Be thou removed, and be thou cast into the sea; and shall not doubt in his heart, but shall believe that those things which he saith shall come to pass; he shall have whatsoever he saith," (Mark 11:23).

Everything on the earth is made up of atoms. Atoms contain electrons. Electrons are made of energy, vibration and frequency.

That is how God created matter in The Beginning.

Matter will *respond* to your instructions.

Why I Am So Sure About This.

How do I know it works?

As soon as my wife and I discovered this, we started to apply this principle and our lives are being *revolutionized*. Not only are we benefiting from this principle, but there are thousands of very successful people around the world that are using these same

Invoke A Blessing On Yourself.

principles to amass great wealth and receive what they want.

The wealthy and successful, do not want to share this type of information, because they do not want the competition.

But God *expects* you to prosper and be blessed.

> Beloved, I Wish Above All Things That Thou Mayest Prosper And Be In Health, Even As Thy Soul Prospers.
>
> - 3 John 1:2

If you study the public education system, you will discover that their goal is to raise masses of *workers*, not a wealthy generation. However, the wealthy pass on this hidden information to their children and very close family members. Average people may stumble upon this secret and achieve great things as well.

As a child of God, The Father, wants you blessed in *all* aspects of your life. That is one of the reasons He sent Jesus to the earth to purchase our salvation, our health and give us a full life of abundance, not of struggle.

Jesus declared, "I came that they may have and enjoy life, and have it in abundance, to the full, till it overflows," (John 10:10 AMP).

Invoke A Blessing On Yourself.

Jesus came so you could...*invoke a blessing on yourself.*

Invoke A Blessing On Yourself.

12

Why Did Abraham Have To Change His Name?

Abraham is considered the father of faith.

The name Abram meant "*exalted* father;"

Then God changed his name to Abraham, "father of a *great* multitude."

"Now the LORD had said unto Abram, Get thee out of thy country, and from thy kindred, and from thy father's house, unto a land that I will shew thee:

And I will make of thee a great nation, and I will bless thee, and make thy name great; and thou shalt be a blessing:

Invoke A Blessing On Yourself.

A GOOD Name Is Rather To Be Chosen Than Great Riches.

-Proverbs 22:1

Invoke A Blessing On Yourself.

And I will bless them that bless thee, and curse him that curseth thee: and in thee shall all families of the earth be blessed.

So Abram departed, as the LORD had spoken unto him; and Lot went with him: and Abram was seventy and five years old when he departed out of Haran," (Genesis 12:1-4).

"After these things the word of the LORD came unto Abram in a vision, saying, Fear not, Abram: I am thy Shield, and thy exceeding great Reward.

And Abram said, LORD God, what wilt Thou give me, seeing I go childless, and the steward of my house is this Eliezer of Damascus?

And Abram said, Behold, to me Thou hast given no seed: and, lo, one born in my house is mine heir.

And, behold, the word of the LORD came unto him, saying, This shall not be thine heir; but he that shall come forth out of thine own bowels shall be thine heir.

And He brought him forth abroad, and said, Look now toward heaven, and tell the stars, if thou be able to number them: and He said unto him, So shall thy seed be.

And he believed in the LORD; and He counted it to him for righteousness." Genesis 15:1-6

Abram tried "helping" God to bring to pass what was promised. "And Sarai said unto Abram, Behold now, the Lord hath restrained me from bearing: I pray thee, go

Invoke A Blessing On Yourself.

in unto my maid; it may be that I may obtain children by her. And Abram hearkened to the voice of Sarai," (Genesis 16:2).

Abram fathered a son from a servant. This is what the Angel of the Lord said about their son in. "And he will be a wild man; his hand will be against every man, and every man's hand against him; and he shall dwell in the presence of all his brethren," (Genesis 16:12).

Later on we read, "And when Abram was ninety years old and nine, the LORD appeared to Abram, and said unto him, I am the Almighty God; walk before Me, and be thou perfect.

"And I will make My covenant between Me and thee, and will multiply thee exceedingly.

"And Abram fell on his face: and God talked with him, saying,

"As for me, behold, My covenant is with thee, and thou shalt be a father of many nations.

"Neither shall thy name any more be called Abram, but thy name shall be Abraham; for a father of many nations have I made thee.

"And I will make thee exceeding fruitful, and I will make nations of thee, and kings shall come out of thee.

"And I will establish My covenant between Me and thee and thy seed after thee in their generations for an

Invoke A Blessing On Yourself.

everlasting covenant, to be a God unto thee, and to thy seed after thee.

"And I will give unto thee, and to thy seed after thee, the land wherein thou art a stranger, all the land of Canaan, for an everlasting possession; and I will be their God.

"And God said unto Abraham, Thou shalt keep My covenant therefore, thou, and thy seed after thee in their generations," (Genesis 17:1-9).

So, the next morning Abraham comes out to get his newspaper. His neighbor yells, "Good morning Abram – Exalted Father!"

Abraham responds, "Good morning neighbor. From now on please do not call me Abram. You will call me Abraham – Father of a great multitude."

The neighbor says, "But to be a father of a great multitude you must have many children."

Abraham then replies, "I will have many children. If you do not call me Abraham, I will not respond to anything else, thank you very much…"

By accepting and celebrating who God says you are, you will…*invoke a blessing on yourself.*

Invoke A Blessing On Yourself.

If You Take The Unchangeable And Use It To Apply Pressure To The Changeable, It Is Obvious Which One Will Yield – The Changeable One. Therefore, When You Apply The Word of God In Faith To This Temporal Realm, Temporal Must Give In And Conform To The Word

—Kenneth Copeland

Invoke A Blessing On Yourself.

13

Choose Faith And Strength; Reject Fear And Unbelief

Receiving *requires* decisiveness.

You must be *determined* to obey when you receive an instruction from God. Here is a great scripture to stand on. "And ye shall serve the LORD your God, and He shall bless thy bread, and thy water; and I will take sickness away from the midst of thee," (Exodus 23:25).

God *wants* you blessed, healthy and strong; as long as you *serve* Him. If you fall away from serving God, you may become so *miserable* that you find yourself running *back* to Him.

Invoke A Blessing On Yourself.

My wife and I believe in *Divine* healing. When friends tell us about 'wonderful' flu shots, drugs and other forms of medication, we do not get excited over it. We respect the medical profession and those who have specialized in it; but we have chosen to *rely* on One Healer. He is The One we have chosen to use...*exclusively*.

Healing is a spiritual transaction that requires *great* faith. Great faith is *unwavering*. It has to be built upon and grown. Sometimes, it is not easy to trust in what you cannot see, but we know that there is more *beyond* our natural 'GPS' screen.

We do not want our children to be exposed to the fear of sickness, and unbelief towards healing, which is found in many hospital environments. Fear is one of the *killers* of The Blessing. We are training our children to learn to trust God when they need a healing. We also strive to live *healthy*; by exercising, eating the right foods, staying in love and staying in The Spirit.

> A Tired Mind Rarely Makes Good Decisions.
>
> -Dr. Mike Murdock

Did you know that every time you get mad or upset, your body releases chemicals that are *harmful* to your body? There is a reason some people look twenty

Invoke A Blessing On Yourself.

years older because they *rarely* smile. Some people are always mad about something.

I would recommend reading *How to Win Friends and Influence People* by Dale Carnegie. Every time you smile or laugh, your body is being healed. When you are feeling sad or tired, just smile and you will notice that you will immediately start the *restorative* process. You never want to stay in a tired, *comatose* state. Dr. Mike Murdock says, "A tired mind rarely makes good decisions."

A doctor said to us, "We are going to give your child this shot."

We replied, "You will not, because we believe in Divine healing."

Do You Trust The Words of A Man Over The Words of Your God?

This may sound weird to some, but when you trust God, it seems strange to see the majority of believers trusting in what a *man* says about their health as the *final* authority on the matter. Many people run to the hospital for any *minor* ailment.

Executives in the medical industry spend millions of dollars, advertizing and promoting their products; hence you see their advertisements in magazines,

Invoke A Blessing On Yourself.

newspapers, on TV, radio, billboards, etc. They want you to *use* their product, because it is a *business*.

You may not need it, but they say you *do*.

You have seen the commercials for yourself.

Someone appears on the screen with an illness. They take a pill and *instantly*, they feel better. There is hardly any commercial that motivates you to call upon The Name of The Lord.

There is no financial *profit* in a message like that.

Pharmaceutical companies *have* to make *money*.

What about praying to The Father in The Name of Jesus next time you are feeling ill? *He is The Healer.* If God said, "I will put none of these diseases upon thee, which I have brought upon the Egyptians: for I am the LORD that healeth thee," (Exodus 15:26).

A Shot of Sickness...To Heal A Sickness.

Why would you allow a shot of 'sickness' in the form of a drug into your body? Is it so your body would be able to fight the disease? If God said He would put *none* of the different kinds of diseases on you, then do not allow the doctors to do it to you.

Praying in The Spirit will open up your radar screen and pull the answers you *need* from the spiritual realm into your life.

Invoke A Blessing On Yourself.

Praying in The Spirit is what *birthed* this book.

Praying in The Spirit will increase your faith and strength. Praying in The Spirit will...*invoke a blessing on yourself.*

Invoke A Blessing On Yourself.

When You Believe The Word, Your Faith Joins With His Faith, The Power of That Word Is Released, The Holy Spirit Goes into Action, And The Word Explodes Into This Natural Realm Becoming A Reality In Your Life.

-Kenneth Copeland

Invoke A Blessing On Yourself.

14

Decree A Thing And It Shall Be Established Unto You

What you say determines what you *experience*.

A new believer sought counsel from a man of God about the difficulty he was having trying to *quit* smoking. The man of God gave him instructions. "Every time you are in the store buying a pack of cigars say to yourself, 'Thank You Jesus for redeeming me from smoking.' When you go outside and get into your car, go ahead and light up that stogie and say, 'Thank You Jesus for redeeming me from smoking.'

"Take a puff of that thing and say, 'Thank You Jesus for redeeming me from smoking.' Take another

Invoke A Blessing On Yourself.

puff and say, 'Thank You Jesus for redeeming me from smoking.' Take another one and another one and every time you take a puff say, 'Thank You Jesus for redeeming me from smoking.' When you finish with one say, 'Thank You Jesus for redeeming me from smoking.'

"Every time you think of smoking or start smoking say, 'Thank You Jesus for redeeming me from smoking.'"

It Happened For This New Believer...

Several weeks later, the new believer returned to the man of God, and informed him that he had been following his instructions. He had made it a habit to say, "Thank You Jesus for redeeming me from smoking."

Eventually, after saying it so many times, this new believer became *persuaded* that he did not need to smoke anymore. After a while, his body no longer had the desire for smoking, and short time later, it became *disgusting* to him.

It is all about what you really, really want...or something you really, really do not want.

Like a laser beam, *focus* your attention and accomplish great feats, by using what you already have; your *mind*, your *spirit*, your *emotions* and your *tongue*.

Invoke A Blessing On Yourself.

> When Your Heart Decides The Destination, Your Mind Will Design A Map To Reach It.
>
> -Dr. Mike Murdock

The secret to change lies in the picture you are drawing in your Mind. *Rename* your situation. Call it what you *want* it to be...not what it *currently* is.

Keep saying what you want, not what you do not.

Your Mind is *visual*.

Never say, "I want to lose weight." Your Mind will see a *picture* of weight. Instead declare, "I want to be healthy."

Never say, "I do not want to stay in a bad marriage." Say, "I want my marriage to improve and become better." The picture in your Mind will be one of an improved marriage...*a better marriage.*

Always stay *positive* and you will get positive results, but if you stay *negative* you will keep getting negative results.

You will *get* what you keep thinking about *most* of the time. Think positive, think what you want, and do not keep acknowledging what you do not have. You may know a person that is critical of *everything* around them; they only see negativity all around them.

Invoke A Blessing On Yourself.

If they get a day off from work, their complaint is, "Now we have to work overtime since we are behind schedule." Instead, they could be grateful for having a day off and earning more money as a result.

If they get a raise, they complain that they now have to pay *more* taxes.

You will never be able to come into agreement on anything with a person like that. If you want to go left they want to go *right*; and next time you want to go right, now they want to go *left*. "A double minded man is unstable in all his ways," (James 1:8).

You Will Simply Attract More of Who You Are.

A pastor who is educated will attract an educated audience. If a pastor does not have a degree, but is very good in the ministry, he will usually attract working class people. A person who is consistently negative will attract more negativity.

Like attracts *like*.

Positive attracts *positive*.

Negative attracts *negative*.

Your friends will be attracted to you because of similarities. It is hard to be attracted to someone who has nothing in common with you.

Invoke A Blessing On Yourself.

There is a popular saying, "A mother's job is never done." Yet, I know mothers who have six to eight children, and are very *positive* and pleasant to be around. It is a blessing to be raised in such a peaceful environment. On the contrary, there are mothers with one or two children, who *complain* about everything.

If this observation applies to you, my intention is not to upset you; but I hope this will be a *wakeup* call.

Always Remember, Someone Has It Worse Than You.

Long time ago, my wife and I attempted to develop a friendship with a certain couple.

The time we spent with them was *never* enjoyable.

After we left their house, or after they left ours, we would feel *drained*.

The conversation was always about them; how they would do this and how they would do that. Since they already knew 'everything,' the conversation was always one-sided. We owned our own successful business and lived in our own house. This couple was always broke and rented their home, yet they never asked, "What do you think we should do to be successful?"

Invoke A Blessing On Yourself.

We are all *still* growing and learning, but when you talk to someone who has accomplished *more* than you, you must ask questions in order to learn from them.

> Questions Host Answers On The Earth.
> -Dr. Mike Murdock

You may be wondering, "If I feel terrible and someone asks how I am doing, should I lie?"

No, do not lie; but do not tell them you feel terrible, sleepy, or tired either. Do not bring a curse on your body; speak blessing over your body.

Say what you want. *Stay in faith.*

Tell them, "I am OK, but I am getting better."

Once you graduate to the next level of health or manifestation, you can tell them, "I am good, but I am getting better by the minute."

You decide what you want for yourself.

No one else can decide it for you. "For this reason I am telling you, whatever you ask for in prayer, believe (trust and be confident) that it is granted to you, and you will get it," (Mark 11:24, AMP).

Sometimes people do not embrace this principle, because speaking their pain *attracts* sympathy; hugs, kisses and pity parties.

Invoke A Blessing On Yourself.

If they declare, "I am good and getting better by the minute," their friends will look at them strangely. They will not receive the *comfort* hug. "Oh, you poor thing. I am so sorry."

If you want to live pitifully the rest of your life, it is your choice; my job here is to show you an option. My Assignment in this book is to help get you out of Egypt and into The Promise Land; without griping and complaining.

The Unthankful Are Always The Unhappy. Ingratitude Is A Cancer That Will Cut Off 80% of Blessings In Your Life.

-Dr. Mike Murdock

Smile and be happy.

Be grateful for what you have.

Find something to be thankful for, surely you are not in a worse situation than other people.

Your gratitude will...*invoke a blessing on yourself.*

Invoke A Blessing On Yourself.

Invoke Discipline And Instruction To Your Children And They Will Be A Joy And Delight To You.

-Yuri I. Tereshchenko

Invoke A Blessing On Yourself.

15

Your Children Are A Heritage From The Lord

Children are a *blessing* from The Lord.

Our two children are very important to me and my wife. We see our children as our *Future*. "Behold, children are a heritage from the Lord, the fruit of the womb a reward," (Psalm 127:3).

We are blessed when we raise them to be a blessing. I come from a family of four boys and four girls. I am conscious that it took our parents a lot of hard work to raise *quality* children.

Invoke A Blessing On Yourself.

In the raising of your children, it is critical to have Jesus, to be Spirit Filled and to hear The Voice of The Holy Spirit.

When I think of quality, I remember a story told by Zig Ziglar during a motivational conference. Many years ago, their company made a basic decision. It would be easier to explain the price for quality *once,* than to apologize for poor quality *forever.*

Go Outside And Speak A Blessing Over Your Son!

Today, I devoted half the day to my family at the pool. As I write this, my wife and our daughter are out shopping. My son and I are at home. My son is outside riding his two wheel scooter where I can watch him as I work.

The Holy Spirit just prompted me to go outside and speak a blessing over our six year old son, to lay my hands on him and pray for him that he would be safe.

Jesus "took them [the children up one by one] in His arms and fervently **invoked** a blessing, placing His hands upon them," (Mark 10:16 AMP).

I want to be like Jesus. Jesus laid His hands on the children to invoke a blessing on them, so I will do the *same.* So, I went outside and called my son. He came up to me. I told him I wanted to pray for him.

Invoke A Blessing On Yourself.

    I laid my hands on him and prayed for his safety, that he would be blessed and angels would protect him everywhere he went. As soon as I got back inside the house, a young girl from the neighborhood came out with another friend, and of course my six year old followed them.

    I could not see him for a few minutes, so I went outside to find him. I noticed that he was playing with the girls on the road. It is not really a safe place for him to be, because of the passing cars, but I felt confident that The Holy Spirit prompted me to pray for my son's safety because he was going to be playing on the road.

It's Better To Build Boys And Girls Than To Mend Men And Women.

-Dr. James C. Dobson

    We *teach* our children the power of prayer.

    When they need something, we have taught them to pray. When they hurt, we have taught them to pray.

    We pray in the morning. We thank God for what we have; for our health, for strength, and for angelic protection over us.

    We pray throughout the day.

    We, most definitely, pray over our food.

Invoke A Blessing On Yourself.

> We teach our children the *value* of The Bible.
> We *listen* to The Bible on CD's. We *read* The Bible.
> All knowledge and wisdom is found in The Bible.

The Bible Is A Book of Divine Instructions For Producing A Fruitful And Successful Life, Thus Proof That God Cares And Loves Us.

-Dr. Mike Murdock

We teach our children to be *thankful*.

When I was growing up, thankfulness was not really taught to me. Learning thankfulness has become a very important process for us. We have started to *count* our blessings. We even have a Blessing Box. Every time we receive a blessing, we write it down on a piece of paper and place it in the box. On Thanksgiving Day, we will read all the blessings we have received.

A scientific study showed that *everything* has a frequency and a vibration, even food. If you say *good* things about the food, the frequency *changes*. You will not notice any change visually, but the food changes frequency. If you say something negative about the food, it will have a negative frequency. That is the reason we *pray* over our food.

Invoke A Blessing On Yourself.

Despite the scientific evidence, most Christian believers want to understand everything from a Biblical point of view. To the skeptical brother or sister, I would like to challenge you to speak bad things over your food before you eat it and see what happens!

Anything Permitted Increases; Conduct Permitted Is Conduct Taught; Never Complain About What You Permit.

-Dr. Mike Murdock

We pray over our food in *thankfulness* to our Father. We speak a blessing over it. As we were growing up, my father shared with us an interesting story. It happened during the war, in a village in Ukraine. A family got together around a table for a meal and the wife asked the husband to bless and thank The Lord for the food. In front of all their children, the husband and father of the house said, "No, I will not thank God for this food, because during these hard times God has not done anything for us. I have to work very hard to earn this food, so I earned it and I deserve all the praise."

The family stood there around the table. They were shocked. A minute or two later, the soldiers barged into the house, grabbed the man, and they were *gone*.

Invoke A Blessing On Yourself.

The family, without their father, bowed their heads, and with tears in their eyes, thanked God for their protection and for the *small* amount of food they had to survive through the night.

Taking a moment to thank God, with your family, for what you have, whether it is a little or a lot, will...*invoke a blessing over yourself.*

Invoke A Blessing On Yourself.

16

A Willing Heart

Servanthood *easily* flows from a *willing* heart.

Abraham sent his eldest servant to find a wife for Isaac, his son. "And the servant took ten camels of the camels of his master, and departed; for all the goods of his master were in his hand: and he arose, and went to Mesopotamia, unto the city of Nahor.

"And he made his camels to kneel down without the city by a well of water at the time of the evening, even the time that women go out to draw water.

"And he said O LORD God of my master Abraham, I pray Thee, send me good speed this day, and shew kindness unto my master Abraham.

Invoke A Blessing On Yourself.

*Everything Is A Seed.
Even A Seed of Nothing Will
Bring A Harvest of Nothing.*

–Dr. Mike Murdock

Invoke A Blessing On Yourself.

"Behold, I stand here by the well of water; and the daughters of the men of the city come out to draw water:

"And let it come to pass, that the damsel to whom I shall say, Let down thy pitcher, I pray Thee, that I may drink; and she shall say, Drink, and I will give thy camels drink also: let the same be she that Thou hast appointed for Thy servant Isaac; and thereby shall I know that Thou hast shewed kindness unto my master.

"And it came to pass, before he had done speaking, that, behold, Rebekah came out, who was born to Bethuel, son of Milcah, the wife of Nahor, Abraham's brother, with her pitcher upon her shoulder.

"And the damsel was very fair to look upon, a virgin, neither had any man known her: and she went down to the well, and filled her pitcher, and came up.

"And the servant ran to meet her, and said, let me, I pray thee, drink a little water of thy pitcher.

"And she said, Drink, my lord: and she hasted, and let down her pitcher upon her hand, and gave him drink.

"And when she had done giving him drink, she said, I will draw water for thy camels also, until they have done drinking.

"And she hasted, and emptied her pitcher into the trough, and ran again unto the well to draw water, and drew for all his camels.

Invoke A Blessing On Yourself.

"And the man wondering at her held his peace, to wit whether the LORD had made his journey prosperous or not.

"And it came to pass, as the camels had done drinking, that the man took a golden earring of half a shekel weight, and two bracelets for her hands of ten shekels weight of gold;" (Genesis 24:10-22).

When Rebekah was asked for some water, she was gracious enough to serve Abraham's servant, and then offer to water his camels as well.

The Bible indicates that she *hasted* to get more water. If you study the process, you will realize that watering the camels was a major task. She changed her schedule because she saw a problem she could *solve*. She was not afraid of the work needed to accomplish this task.

A few hours later, Rebekah found out she had *solved* a problem for the chief steward of the *richest* man alive at that time. She discovered Abraham's servant was looking for a *bride* with a *servant's* heart.

Would You Have Stopped...?

A man in New York was driving to work.

He stopped on the side of the road to help a man change a flat tire on a limousine. This man later found out that Donald Trump, the billionaire, was in the limo.

Invoke A Blessing On Yourself.

In appreciation for his kind deed, Donald Trump paid off the man's mortgage note.

You have to be willing and able to serve...*in the right place at the right time...*

I do not think Rebekah had *naturally* grown up with a servant's heart. I strongly believe someone had to *train* her in adaptation and servanthood. Someone had to *guide* her. I believe it is a vital part of the parent's responsibility to train their children. "Train up a child in the way he should go: and when he is old, he will not depart from it," (Proverbs 22:6).

I do not think it is easy to train *every* child to have a servant's heart, but *most* people can be trained for *greatness*. Training children will require *continuous* encouragement and correction.

Invoke Learning And Keep Learning Because He Who Ceases To Learn Cannot Adequately Teach.

-Yuri I. Tereshchenko

Why is this topic so important?

Part of living the blessed and successful life is having children that are a blessing to you and not a curse. If you invest the time to train up your children, they will grow up and bless you. If you invest your money, your

Invoke A Blessing On Yourself.

energy and everything you are in teaching, encouraging and correcting your children, you will reap many blessings.

One of the most important lessons you will convey to your children is the fear of God...*a healthy fear of sinning against The Almighty God.*

If they fear God it will be easier for them to *honor* the laws of the land. If they fear God it will be easy for them to *listen* to The Voice of The Holy Spirit. If your child fears God, it will be *harder* for them to sin.

My parents raised us with such a fear of sin, that my wife was the *first* girl I ever kissed at twenty one years of age. We were both *virgins* when we got married.

Having a willing heart...*will invoke a blessing on yourself.*

Invoke A Blessing On Yourself.

17

Honor

Honor is vital to your *future* success.

Teach your children to honor elders, to honor their parents, to honor people who are higher in authority, and to honor their peers.

Teach them to be comfortable in *any* environment.

Teach them not to complain, but to *be grateful*.

> A Child Who Knows How To Pray, Work, And Think Is Already Half-Educated.
> - Croft M. Pentz

Teach them to *love* The Word of God and to pray.

Invoke A Blessing On Yourself.

When A General Gives A Command, It Is An Act of Dishonor To Question Why.

-Yuri I. Tereshchenko

Invoke A Blessing On Yourself.

I was always taught that you can have *anything*, if you work *hard* enough. That may not always be true, but hard work has now become a part of me. I am not afraid of work. I *enjoy* working. I enjoy working *smart*, not just working hard.

Your eyes and your ears are *gates*.

What do you *allow* into your gates? What TV programs do you allow in your home? Not all children's programs are for children. Many are the works of the devil to *teach* rebellion, deception and wickedness.

Everything should point toward *Jesus*.

Everything should have a *Biblical* connotation.

Our spirit is like a sponge. Whatever you feed it will be *absorbed*; and when you get squeezed, whatever has been absorbed will come *out*.

A Lesson To Learn From The Amish.

A great example for training up a child comes from the Amish. When they train a horse they expect it to learn *focus* and *obedience*, because the whole family will be riding in the carriage pulled by that horse. When the Amish have to ride their carriage through town, alongside automobiles, the horse has to be focused and obedient. One wrong move could get the family injured or killed.

The same principle applies to raising a child.

Invoke A Blessing On Yourself.

The goal is to train up the child to be focused and obedient. "Train up a child in the way he should go: and when he is old, he will not depart from it," (Proverbs 22:6).
Never train your child to *react* to yelling.
If you have to yell every time you have something important to say, you will be forced to scream, just to get a *simple* message across. You will probably end up frustrated *most* of the time.
When your children become adults, they will need to relearn what you taught them, because their boss may not yell at them, but instead *quietly* ask them to permanently leave their place of employment. It is better to learn this simple lesson earlier than later.

What You Expect Is What You Get. Make Sure You Invoke Positive Expectations On Yourself.

-Nadia A. Tereshchenko

Your child needs to respond to a *normal* tone of voice. Only on very rare occasions, like when there is *imminent* danger, say from a car on the street, should you use a loud voice. Raise your voice only for urgency. If yelling is normal, you will not have an option when you need to communicate in an emergency.

Invoke A Blessing On Yourself.

You cannot train with shouts and expect a *whisper* to be obeyed.

Sculpture An Environment of Honor.

Treating one another with Honor is vital to creating a peaceful home environment. When you get home, you should enter a castle of protection; where you feel safe, where you can let your guard down, relax and kick up your feet.

It is refreshing to know that your home is where you are loved and where you will not be hurt intentionally. Our home is where we have created a stress free environment for our children to grow and develop.

In nature, hyper-communication has been successfully applied for as long as the earth has existed. The organized flow of life among insects proves this dramatically. Modern man knows it on a much more subtle level as "intuition."

Stress, worry or a hyperactive mind sends a *negative* signal. Negative signals *stifle* creativity and great ideas. Negative signals *sabotage* hyper-communication.

When a queen ant is separated from her colony, the remaining worker ants will *continue* building fervently according to plan. However, if the queen is killed, all work in the colony stops. No ant will know what to do.

Invoke A Blessing On Yourself.

Apparently, the queen *transmits* the 'building plans' even from a distance - via the group consciousness with her subjects. As long as she is alive, she can be as far away as she wants and still communicate.

Our human nature is not like that of animals, but parents can train children to be successful, through example and opportunity. Furthermore, if parents are *dependent* on controlled substances, or have another kind of *addiction* or sin in their life, their children, by default, will be affected by that negative environment.

Pray for your children.
Bless your children.
Plead The Blood of Jesus over them.
Pray angelic *protection* over them.

Angels are not naked babies; they are *mighty* beings ready to hearken to your command as you *declare* The Word of The Lord over your family. "Bless the Lord, ye His angels, that excel in strength, that do His commandments, hearkening unto the voice of His word," (Psalm 103:20).

Everything You Do Affects Your Child's Development.

While our children are young, we strive to do everything as a family. After they have grown up, we

Invoke A Blessing On Yourself.

may not have the same opportunity as we do now. When we take vacations, we plan to spend as much time as possible with them.

Your children are your *investment*, your *future* and your *heritage*. "Lo, children are an heritage of the Lord: and the fruit of the womb is His reward," (Psalm 127:3). "Thy wife shall be as a fruitful vine by the sides of thine house: thy children like olive plants round about thy table," (Psalm 128:3).

As you demonstrate Honor to your family, you will...*invoke a blessing on yourself.*

Invoke A Blessing On Yourself.

Invoke Excellence In Your Life; Do Small Things In A Great Way, Then You Can Achieve Great Things.

-Yuri I. Tereshchenko

Invoke A Blessing On Yourself.

18

EXCELLENCE

My goal is to *always* achieve Excellence.

All through our 11 years of marriage, I have *always* conveyed Excellence to my wife. Excellence is hard and costly. Sometimes you get weary of maintaining Excellence, but at the end of the day you realize you have a chance to start over and begin a *new* day.

Your upbringing or training will drive you toward or away from Excellence. My father always trained us to be punctual. Many people come to work *casually*. Some people chronically arrive at the last minute or *late*.

I *despise* tardiness. Even when I do not feel like making an appointment, I like to arrive early; because I believe that if you are late in the *spirit*, you are late in the *natural*.

Invoke A Blessing On Yourself.

Whatever you train your child to be, is what they will stick to. "Train up a child in the way he should go: and when he is old, he will not depart from it," (Proverbs 22:6).
Invest in your child.
Give your children the *best* education you can afford. Strive for Excellence and it will pay off with *great* dividends for you.

The Qualities of A Mother Matter...Greatly.

The qualities of a mother make a *lasting* impression on a child. Someone said, "A hand that rocks the cradle, rules the world."
While I am at work, I rely *heavily* on my wife to teach our children throughout the day. During work days I only have a few hours in the evenings with them. My wife is *training* them for the Future, so I attend to her knowing she attends to our children.

Excellence Is A Widely Desired...But Rare Quality.

Never settle for anything less than Excellence.
I am determined to have Excellence in my home. I will not have old worn out furniture. I will not sit on old dirty chairs. I will not eat from a dirty table.

Invoke A Blessing On Yourself.

Some people may have grown up in a village somewhere or in an environment where they were not exposed to Excellence for whatever reason. Their perspective of a clean house would be different. If they walked barefooted on dirt roads or grew up around animals, it would be harder to have a neat house.

I grew up in a family of 8 children; 4 girls and 4 boys. Our parents would discipline us with a belt when we disobeyed. They instilled a healthy *fear* in us. If I washed the floor half-heartedly, I got a beating. When we made our beds, they had to look neat. When we were instructed to do something, we had to act promptly, otherwise we got reprimanded.

I Am Thankful For My Upbringing.

I am glad I had a semi-military upbringing.

I now have a good understanding of what a clean car is, both inside and out. I appreciate having a clean home, with all the dishes washed. I am glad to have a home without piles of clothing all over the place.

After our wedding, I kept emphasizing to my wife that everything had to be neat and orderly. We had a lot of fights, because to her, a pile of dirty dishes in the sink was a clean kitchen, because the dishes were not all over

Invoke A Blessing On Yourself.

the dinner table. To me a pile of dirty dishes was just *another* pile.

We had a *different* perception of clean.

The carpet, if vacuumed once a week, was clean to her. To me, a clean carpet was one that was vacuumed *daily*. As I am writing this book, we have been married for eleven years. I keep brainwashing her about Excellence.

I have a great wife. She has come a long way from where she was and so have I; it has been a great learning experience for the both of us. I kept telling her that I will have Excellence even if I had to sleep less, get an additional job and work extra hours; but praise God, now I do not need to do any of that. We are blessed and we keep applying the principles in this book and we...*invoke blessings on ourselves.*

> But As Many As Received Him, To Them Gave He Power To Become The Sons of God, Even To Them That Believe On His Name.
>
> -John 1:12

We teach our children that we are *different*.
We are not better than others, we are just different.
We are *royalty*. What others may do, we may not.

Invoke A Blessing On Yourself.

We are Overcomers, we are Extraordinary, we are Uncommon, and we walk in the Kingly Anointing.

Again, I do not want to convey that we are better than others, but as a child of The Most High God, YOU should have the same expectation and perception of *yourself*.

Speak to yourself.
You are *Excellent*.
You are an *Overcomer*.
You are *Extraordinary*.
You are *Uncommon*.
You walk in *The Kingly Anointing*.

Proclaim it. *Act* like a king or queen. Do not be rude and obnoxious because of your anointing.

Walk with Authority, but stay *honorable*.

You will be blessed. "And the LORD shall make thee the head, and not the tail; and thou shalt be above only, and thou shalt not be beneath; if that thou hearken unto the commandments of the LORD thy God, which I command thee this day, to observe and to do them" (Deuteronomy 28:13).

Get this picture of yourself...and live *into* it.

The reason you are reading this book is you want to experience and possess all these things in your life; and that is why you will...*invoke a blessing on yourself.*

Invoke A Blessing On Yourself.

You Can Deceive Some People Some of The Time; But You Can't Deceive All The People All The Time.
          -Dr. John C. Maxwell

Invoke A Blessing On Yourself.

19

Deception Is Not Beneficial For Your Health...Or For Your Future Success...

Deception is *costly*.

Jacob *stole* his brother's blessing through deception. "And he said, Is not he rightly named Jacob? for he hath supplanted me these two times: he took away my birthright; and, behold, now he hath taken away my blessing. And he said, Hast thou not reserved a blessing for me?" (Genesis 27:36).

Jacob had to run from his brother. He left home and fled to Haran. "Now therefore, my son, obey my voice; and arise, flee thou to Laban my brother to Haran;

Invoke A Blessing On Yourself.

And tarry with him a few days, until thy brother's fury turn away," (Genesis 27:43-44).

After Jacob worked for seven years to get Rachel as his wife, Laban, her father, *tricked* him. The morning after his wedding day, Jacob woke up to find Leah, Rachel's older sister, in his bed.

"And Jacob served seven years for Rachel; and they seemed unto him but a few days, for the love he had to her. And Jacob said unto Laban, Give me my wife, for my days are fulfilled, that I may go in unto her...And it came to pass, that in the morning, behold, it was Leah: and he said to Laban, What is this thou hast done unto me? did not I serve with thee for Rachel? wherefore then hast thou beguiled me?" (Genesis 29:20-21, 25).

When You Sow Deception You Will Reap Deception.

Jacob had to work *another* seven years to get Rachel. "Fulfil her week, and we will give thee this also for the service which thou shalt serve with me yet seven other years. And Jacob did so, and fulfilled her week: and he gave him Rachel his daughter to wife also," (Genesis 29:27-28).

In Genesis 31:41-42 (AMP), Jacob says to Laban, "I have been twenty years in your house. I served you fourteen years for your two daughters and six years for

Invoke A Blessing On Yourself.

your flocks; and you have changed my wages ten times. And if the God of my father, the God of Abraham and the Dread [lest he should fall] and Fear [lest he offend] of Isaac, had not been with me, surely you would have sent me away now empty-handed. God has seen my affliction and humiliation and the [wearying] labor of my hands and rebuked you last night."

Become A Person of Integrity.

If you ever want to become blessed, successful and wealthy, become a person of integrity.

You will need God on *your* side.

If you offer a product or service without integrity, you will have a hard time becoming successful. People will *not* buy your product.

If we go to buy something and my wife says, "I do not feel good about this person," most of the time we will not make the purchase.

When we deal with a person who is cordial and pleasant, we want to sow favor into their life; by giving them a *discount* if we are selling, or by paying the *full* asking price if we are buying.

We choose to *celebrate* their good spirit.

Invoke A Blessing On Yourself.

It is always a pleasure to deal with a pleasant, caring person. You can invoke many blessings just by smiling and being nice.

Are you deceiving yourself or your soul?

When you act against your conscience, your body generates *cancer* cells. Not only are you hurting someone else, you are most definitely hurting *yourself*.

Be *happy*.
Be *honest*.
Be *diligent*.
Be *organized*.
That will help you...*invoke your blessing*.

Why Do Some People Enjoy More Favor Than Others?

Your integrity will always be remembered *longer* than your product. If people perceive they were misled into purchasing your product or service, you will not be successful.

Your business will *struggle*.

Why do some people get more attention than others? Because, it is hard to *hide* trustworthiness and it is difficult to *conceal* integrity.

Invoke A Blessing On Yourself.

Deception Will Birth Pain.

I have a friend who was purchasing a business.

He invested his time, energy and money preparing to take over the business. The contractual agreement called for certain things to be done a *specific* way. The seller thought he was smarter than my friend, so at the last minute he decided to *amend* some components of the contract.

The deal fell through, because some questionable items were added to the contract. That last act of 'slither' broke the deal. The contract was voided and the deal was lost. I was glad my friend was able to get out of the deal.

There were too many *loopholes* in the contract.

If You Could Kick The Person Responsible For Most of Your Troubles, You Would Not Be Able To Sit Down For Weeks.

-Unknown

In the book, *The Art of Influence,* by Chris Widener there is a story about a $50 Million deal that was on the table. An investor came in, and overheard that the CFO had *lied* about sending out a letter. The investor decided not to invest in the deal because of that *one* lie.

Invoke A Blessing On Yourself.

The moral of the story was that if you lie in the *small* stuff, there is no guarantee that you will not lie with the *big* things.

Consistent lying does not make you a liar. One lie makes you a liar. Can you be trusted with the little things? The Bible says that if we are *faithful* in small things we will be *trusted* with big things. "Well done, thou good and faithful servant: thou hast been faithful over a few things, I will make thee ruler over many things," (Matthew 25:21).

Being a person of habitual integrity will...*invoke a blessing on yourself.*

Invoke A Blessing On Yourself.

20

What You Know And What You Do Not Know

To be successful, you will have to be *teachable*.

> To Know...And Not Invoke or Use The Knowledge...Is Not To Know
>
> –Yuri I. Tereshchenko

Never say, "I know that," or "I got it."
Are you *willing* to admit you don't know what you don't know...and then find out what you don't know?

Invoke A Blessing On Yourself.

To Know...And Not Invoke or Use The Knowledge...Is Not To Know

—Yuri I. Tereshchenko

Invoke A Blessing On Yourself.

As you go through life learning, you will realize *where* you need improvement. Maybe you grew up in a family where lying and deception were a normal part of life, so you would need to *change* your way of thinking.

Do not be concerned about *how* you will change.

Learn to change in the area you need change, and your heart will get you to your destination. As you read this great book and others, your Mind will become renewed.

This is a Biblical principle. "And be not conformed to this world: but be ye transformed by the renewing of your mind," (Romans 12:2).

Renew your Mind.

Get new information.

Replace old negative information with new thoughts. As you receive new thoughts, you will receive new ideas. Just one idea can *change* your life *forever*, so start applying this principle in your life right *now*. Do not wait another moment.

Think on the following quote.

Invoke A Blessing On Yourself.

> We Cannot Control The Parade of Negative Thoughts Marching Through Our Minds. But We Can Choose Which Ones We Will Give Our Attention To. Picture Your Thoughts As People Passing By The Front of Your Home. Just Because They're Walking By Doesn't Mean You Have To Invite Them In.
>
> -Gladys Edmunds

The renewing of your Mind is a *continual* process.

For successful continuation of the process, you must continue to *grow*.

A magnet has a magnetic field which we cannot see, but we *know* exists. That same magnet has *different* polarities; one will *attract* and the other one will *repel*.

In the same manner, each person will attract either the positive or the negative in their life. Your thoughts, your attitude and your actions are like electricity. With electricity you can cook a meal and provide comfort in your home, yet electricity can also harm or kill people.

Philippians 4:8 says, "Whatsoever things are true, whatsoever things are honest, whatsoever things are just, whatsoever things are pure, whatsoever things are lovely, whatsoever things are of good report; if there be any virtue, and if there be any praise, think on these things."

Integrity will make you *proud* of yourself.

Invoke A Blessing On Yourself.

Concentrate on being a person of integrity and Excellence. Think positive. Think about attracting good things. Ask questions and think on...*invoking a blessing on yourself.*

You will find a great story in the book, Think And Grow Rich. A couple sold their farm and spent the next few years searching for riches through gold mining. After having no success, they decided to return to their farm. As they approached their farm, they noticed a tall fence. The area was heavily guarded by the government because *under* their old farm was a goldmine.

They did not have to leave.

If they had stayed, they would have had *more* money than they could spend.

You have a goldmine *within* you.

You might not know how to bring it forth, but that is why you have this and other great books that will help you attract and...*invoke a blessing on yourself.*

Invoke A Blessing On Yourself.

Invoke The Future On Yourself And Decide To Live There.

-Yuri I. Tereshchenko

Invoke A Blessing On Yourself.

21

Sow Into Your Future

Joseph had a *picture* of his Future.

Joseph saw a *dream* about his Future. He did not know *how* it would come to pass, but he had a *picture* of what his Future would *be*.

That picture kept him *motivated*. "For, behold, we were binding sheaves in the field, and, lo, my sheaf arose, and also stood upright; and, behold, your sheaves stood round about, and made obeisance to my sheaf...And he dreamed yet another dream, and told it his brethren, and said, Behold, I have dreamed a dream more; and, behold, the sun and the moon and the eleven stars made obeisance to me," (Genesis 37:7, 9).

Joseph's brothers were *jealous* because they did not believe that Joseph would one day *rule* over them. "And

Invoke A Blessing On Yourself.

his brethren said to him, Shalt thou indeed reign over us? or shalt thou indeed have dominion over us? And they hated him yet the more for his dreams, and for his words," (Genesis 37:8).

In The Midst of Danger, God Scheduled Deliverance.

Joseph's brothers planned to kill him, but God *protected* him. "And when they saw him afar off, even before he came near unto them, they conspired against him to slay him. And they said one to another, Behold, this dreamer cometh. Come now therefore, and let us slay him, and cast him into some pit, and we will say, Some evil beast hath devoured him: and we shall see what will become of his dreams," (Genesis 37:18-20 AMP).

Joseph was sold to Ishmaelites for twenty pieces of silver, taken to Egypt, and then sold to Potiphar, an officer of Pharaoh, and the captain and chief executioner of the royal guard. (See Genesis 37.)

The Bible documents, "The Lord was with Joseph, and he [though a slave] was a successful and prosperous man; and he was in the house of his master the Egyptian," (Genesis 39:2 AMP).

Invoke A Blessing On Yourself.

Potiphar's wife wanted to sleep with Joseph. He had a *choice* to make. He had to decide if he would take what did not belong to him...or if he would resist.

He chose to *resist* the advances of his master's wife.

Joseph Knew The Power of Integrity.

He said to Potiphar's wife, "See here, with me in the house my master has concern about nothing; he has put all that he has in my care. He is not greater in this house than I am; nor has he kept anything from me except you, for you are his wife. How then can I do this great evil and sin against God?" (Genesis 39:8-9 AMP).

Can you imagine how much power, authority and trust Joseph had earned by that time? Integrity is a rare thing, but Joseph was a person of *high* integrity.

Joseph knew the *importance* of integrity.

Time after time, Joseph resisted the advances of Potiphar's wife. "And it came to pass, as she spake to Joseph day by day, that he hearkened not unto her, to lie by her, or to be with her," (Genesis 39:10).

One day she became so upset with Joseph for resisting her, that she deceived Potiphar into throwing Joseph into prison. "And she spake unto him according to these words, saying, The Hebrew servant, which thou hast brought unto us, came in unto me to mock me: And

Invoke A Blessing On Yourself.

it came to pass, as I lifted up my voice and cried, that he left his garment with me, and fled out. And it came to pass, when his master heard the words of his wife, which she spake unto him, saying, After this manner did thy servant to me; that his wrath was kindled. And Joseph's master took him, and put him into the prison, a place where the king's prisoners were bound: and he was there in the prison," (Genesis 39:17-20).

Joseph must have had discouraging thoughts, but we do not read anywhere that Joseph complained. "But the Lord was with Joseph, and showed him mercy and loving-kindness and gave him favor in the sight of the warden of the prison," (Genesis 39:21 AMP).

Through all this Joseph was *tested* and *prepared* for his destiny. "He sent a man before them, even Joseph, who was sold for a servant...Until the time that his word came: the word of the Lord tried him," (Psalm 105:17, 19).

Grumbling And Complaining Will Sabotage Your Blessing.

Murmuring and complaining will not help you *get* a blessing, *become* blessed or *stay* blessed. Here is what The Bible says about it in Jude 1, "Look! The Master comes with thousands of holy angels to bring judgment against them all, convicting each person of every defiling act of

Invoke A Blessing On Yourself.

shameless sacrilege, of every dirty word they have spewed of their pious filth." These are the "grumpers," the bellyachers, grabbing for the biggest piece of the pie, talking big, saying anything they think will get them ahead," (Jude 14-16, The Message Bible).

As the children of Israel migrated to Canaan from Egypt, it is the *gripers* who got the *vipers*. "And the people spake against God, and against Moses, Wherefore have ye brought us up out of Egypt to die in the wilderness? for there is no bread, neither is there any water; and our soul loatheth this light bread. And the Lord sent fiery serpents among the people, and they bit the people; and much people of Israel died," (Numbers 21:5-6).

The Missionary And The Snake.

I remember the story of a missionary in the jungle.

He was sleeping in a small hut. In the middle of the night a large snake fell through the roof and landed right on top of the missionary's chest. The missionary had many thoughts. He was upset that, instead of *rewarding* him, God would *allow* a snake to kill him.

A short time passed, but it seemed like an eternity.

Suddenly, two men stormed his hut with the intention of killing him. The snake bit the two men then

Invoke A Blessing On Yourself.

slithered *back* into the jungle. The Missionary's attitude became *different* toward God.

Griping and complaining will kill a good *attitude* and eventually destroy a great *Future*.

That is one of the reasons I referenced Joseph.

Even in tough situations, stay *positive, trust* God and *visualize* your Future.

In some parts of Mexico, hot and cold springs are found side by side. The women often boil their clothes in the hot springs and rinse them in the cold springs. A tourist, who had been watching this process, remarked to his Mexican friend, "I guess they think God is very generous."

"Oh no, Señor," he replied. "There is a lot of grumbling because He supplies no soap for us!"

Joseph Constantly Sowed Toward His Future.

While Joseph was in prison, Pharaoh's butler and baker were imprisoned there as well. Joseph noticed their sadness and depression. Joseph was able to interpret their dreams and what he declared over them came to pass within a few days.

The butler and the baker were both released from prison; but only one lived to carry his message to Pharaoh. "And he restored the chief butler unto his

Invoke A Blessing On Yourself.

butlership again; and he gave the cup into Pharaoh's hand: But he hanged the chief baker: as Joseph had interpreted to them," (Genesis 40:21-22.)

"And there was there with us a young man, an Hebrew, servant to the captain of the guard; and we told him, and he interpreted to us our dreams; to each man according to his dream he did interpret. And it came to pass, as he interpreted to us, so it was; me he restored unto mine office, and him he hanged. Then Pharaoh sent and called Joseph, and they brought him hastily out of the dungeon: and he shaved himself, and changed his raiment, and came in unto Pharaoh," (Genesis 41:12-14).

All the while, in *every* situation, Joseph was sowing into his Future. Sowing into your Future will...*invoke the blessing on yourself.*

Invoke A Blessing On Yourself.

Give Me Five Minutes With A Person's Checkbook, And I Will Tell You Where Their Heart Is.

-Billy Graham

Invoke A Blessing On Yourself.

22

Finances

God blesses *every* act of obedience.

I remember when we sowed a very nice car into the life of a young pastor God was raising up. After I gave him the keys I got into my truck, ready to go home. Then I had a thought, "What if I missed God? Should I have waited? Maybe I should have prayed more?"

The Voice of The Holy Spirit replied to my spirit, "Everything you do in order to be obedient to Me will be rewarded." Even if you miss it, I believe God will bless you. A Seed sown as a 'sacrifice' brings dividends.

Everything you do will affect your Future.

Every thought, every word, every action and every single decision will affect your Future.

Invoke A Blessing On Yourself.

Spend Your Money Wisely...For A Peaceful Life.

Your finances will *affect* your Future.

Only buy what you have the money for; unless it is a big purchase, like a house. Save up the cash to buy your car. If you use your money wisely, your life will be more *peaceful*. It took us three months to find our BMW, but we got an excellent deal and paid cash for it. It has been a great investment for us because we got a discount of 40% off the retail dealer price.

When we bought a bedroom suite it was $5,000 in the furniture store, but it took us about two or three month's to find a great deal on a discontinued model. All pieces were already packed in boxes and we only paid $2,500...*a 50% discount*.

Be smart. Take your time and find a great deal. You will remember it for a long time. Never be in a hurry. Plan, research, ask questions and shop around.

Pray about it.

Is it going to *save* you time or money?

Is it going to *make* you money?

God Does Not Want You Living Paycheck To Paycheck.

Do not buy things just because you can charge them on your credit card or because the bank will give

Invoke A Blessing On Yourself.

you a loan. If you want to buy that nice car, *save* the money, then pay *cash* for it.

The time it will take you to save up for that special purchase will make you *diligent*, it will teach you *sacrifice* and will give you plenty of time to *think* about the Future.

Several months or years down the road, if you are still set on making your purchase, then go ahead and do it. Many people live paycheck to paycheck. That is not what God wants for you. Instead of slowing down and paying off some debt, or building their savings, they would rather have the *latest* gadget.

It is okay to have things, but at what cost.

If you paid for something with cash and got a huge discount, that is great; but if you purchased it with a credit card at 30% interest, that is not financially smart.

Texans have a slogan for such disorder, "Big hat, no cattle." Never buy things just to *look* rich.

Become rich and then buy things *responsibly*.

Get out of debt and stay out of debt, because debt is very rarely a blessing. Sometimes it is better not to have a thing, than to have it and not be at peace.

You will be *happier* without debt.

You may think it would be nice to have that large, luxury automobile, instead learn to *faith* it in. *Believe* for it, *speak* it into existence and it will come to pass.

Invoke A Blessing On Yourself.

One of the best ministries I would recommend for getting out of debt is The Debt Free Army. On their website, *www.debtfreearmy.org,* you can sign up for daily or weekly information that you can apply in your life.

The Debt Free Army Ministry is great ground to sow your Seed into and you will be *significantly* blessed for your association with them.

I know Dr. Harold Herring personally; he is the President of this great Ministry. Our families have a wonderful relationship.

Sowing And Reaping.

Learn to tap into the principle of sowing and reaping. The Bible teaches us that if you sow you will *reap*. "…for whatsoever a man soweth, that shall he also reap," (Galatians 6:7).

Be careful about sowing Seed into *worthless* soil.

Pray…Sow…Believe…Receive is a formula that involves faith, so *build* your faith.

Modern society pushes you towards trying to figure out *how* this formula works. This is where a lot of people fail. Instead of concentrating on the end result, a lot of time is wasted trying to figure out how things work.

Do not be preoccupied with the *how*.

Focus on the *end* result. Believe for your blessings.

Invoke A Blessing On Yourself.

Speak your blessings and they will manifest.

Worry is *negative* goal setting, because you concentrate on the problem and not the solution. When you feel discouraged about something, it may be because you are trying to figure out the how. When your concentration is on the how, your faith will no longer work because your logic has been *engaged*.

Worrying Is Negative Goal-Setting, Because You Concentrate On The Problem And Not The Solution.
-Yuri I. Tereshchenko

When you have a genuine problem, do what you can; and the things you have no control over, *entrust* to The Lord. The only thing you need to say is, "Father, I come to You in The Name of Jesus and here is my problem. I have done everything I could and now I commit this problem into Your hands. Thank You for taking care of it for me. Amen."

Your Mind will keep coming back to the same problem. Just declare this *every* time, "All is well; my Father is taking care of it. It will work out in my favor."

Do not try to reason it out, just follow these instructions single-mindedly. Do not deviate from the

Invoke A Blessing On Yourself.

plan. Avoid double-mindedness. "A double minded man is unstable in all his ways," (James 1:8).

A good man invokes a blessing on himself so his family will be blessed. Poor people are not concerned about transferring wealth to the next generations, but The Bible teaches us to leave money as an inheritance for our children and our grandchildren. "A good man leaveth an inheritance to his children's children," (Proverbs 13:22).

It took Joseph about *20 years* to go from the pit to the palace, so be *patient* and keep expecting those blessings to come in.

Seed, *Time* and *Harvest* are the three phases that you will have to go through to get what you expect.

The *Timing* is dependent on the kind of person you are. The *Harvest* depends on who you are and the Seed you sow. What kind of Seed are you sowing?

A Seed of Nothing, in time, will create a Harvest of Nothing. A great *Seed*, great *attitude* and right *confession* will, in time invoke a *great* Harvest.

That is why you have this book, to be reminded of the steps you can take to...*invoke a blessing on yourself.*

Invoke A Blessing On Yourself.

23

Do You Have The Attitude of A Giant or A Grasshopper?

Victim mentality is *contagious*.

At a time of crisis, most people will talk about how *terrible* things are, because it is so *easy* to have a victim mentality. Talk about how BIG your God is instead of how big your storm is...and always remember - BIG God, little devil.

I read a story about a major earthquake that alarmed the inhabitants of a very small village. One old woman, who was well known in that village, remained

Invoke A Blessing On Yourself.

Your Attitude Determines If You Will Be Granted Access.

-Yuri I. Tereshchenko

Invoke A Blessing On Yourself.

surprisingly calm and joyous. Someone asked her, "Mother why you are not afraid of the earthquake?"

She replied, "I rejoice in knowing I serve a God Who can shake the world."

Whose Report Will You Believe...?

Moses sent twelve men to investigate the land of Canaan. Moses commanded them, "Look the land over, see what it is like. Assess the people: Are they strong or weak? Are there few or many? Observe the land: Is it pleasant or harsh? Describe the towns where they live: Are they open camps or fortified with walls? And the soil: Is it fertile or barren? Are there forests? And try to bring back a sample of the produce that grows there — this is the season for the first ripe grapes," (Numbers 13:18-20, The Message Bible).

"They presented themselves before Moses and Aaron and the whole congregation of the People of Israel in the Wilderness of Paran at Kadesh. They reported to the whole congregation and showed them the fruit of the land. Then they told the story of their trip: "We went to the land to which you sent us and, oh! It does flow with milk and honey! Just look at this fruit! The only thing is that the people who live there are fierce, their cities are

Invoke A Blessing On Yourself.

huge and well fortified. Worse yet, we saw descendants of the giant Anak," (Numbers 13:26-29, The Message).

"Caleb interrupted, called for silence before Moses and said, "Let's go up and take the land — now. We can do it." But the others said, "We can't attack those people; they're way stronger than we are." They spread scary rumors among the People of Israel. They said, "We scouted out the land from one end to the other — it's a land that swallows people whole. Everybody we saw was huge. Why, we even saw the Nephilim giants (the Anak giants come from the Nephilim). Alongside them we felt like grasshoppers. And they looked down on us as if we were grasshoppers," (Numbers 13:30-33, The Message).

What Is Your Response...Faith or Fear?

"And all the congregation lifted up their voice, and cried; and the people wept that night," (Numbers 14:1).

Can you see how words can be so powerful?

The people that heard the report were *full* of fear?

Because of their fear, they started to grumble and complain; they wanted to *replace* their leader and go back to Egypt. Joshua and Caleb, who were among the twelve scouts, rose up and told the people not to be *afraid* and not to *rebel* against The Lord.

Invoke A Blessing On Yourself.

"And all the children of Israel murmured against Moses and against Aaron: and the whole congregation said unto them, Would God that we had died in the land of Egypt! or would God we had died in this wilderness! And they said one to another, Let us make a captain, and let us return into Egypt, (Numbers 14:2, 4).

Joshua and Caleb *encouraged* the people that they could take the land with God's help. "And Joshua the son of Nun, and Caleb the son of Jephunneh, which were of them that searched the land, rent their clothes: And they spake unto all the company of the children of Israel, saying, The land, which we passed through to search it, is an exceeding good land. If the Lord delight in us, then He will bring us into this land, and give it us; a land which floweth with milk and honey. Only rebel not ye against the Lord, neither fear ye the people of the land; for they are bread for us: their defence is departed from them, and the Lord is with us: fear them not," (Numbers 14:6-9).

Whose Report Are You Focused On?

If you always look at what is negative or bad in a situation, your Mind and your spirit will be so *distracted* that, most of the time you will *miss* your blessings and the good things that are right in front of you.

The twelve spies saw Canaan - *the Future of Israel*.

Invoke A Blessing On Yourself.

Ten spies saw the Future and decided *not* to live there...*two spies saw the Future and decided to live there.*
Your decisions will *decide* your Future.

Reality And Attitude.

I heard Zig Ziglar talk about sharing knowledge.
"The reason for sharing good knowledge is to reach down to the ones that don't know, because of sheer numbers they will reach up and pull you down."
There are more grasshoppers than giants, so we have our work cut out for us. You may be saying that we have to face reality, but The Bible teaches us that reality is *first* created by the spiritual world...*or in the spirit.*
All our lives, we were always trained to *face* reality.
That information came from people who were not aware of the fact that you *create* your own reality. Once you are aware of your God given creative power, by thinking and saying what God says; you will have control of your desires and your creative experience.
You created your own reality or someone else created it for you. Some time back, the reality for the labor class in China was created. The rulers of China *controlled* the opium and they wanted to make sure the working class stayed *drugged,* so they would continue to

Invoke A Blessing On Yourself.

stay at the bottom of society, as the working class, while the rich would continue *unchallenged* at the top.

> Gratitude Is The Seed For More.
>
> -Dr. Mike Murdock

Your *attitude* is more important than *reality*.
Your *mind-set* is more important than the *facts*.
Someone may try to *convince* you that you *cannot* succeed at something; but with the *right* attitude you can *achieve* it. Someone may consider you *capable* of success, but if your attitude is not empowering, you will have *difficulty* believing that you can.

One of the *greatest* attitudes you can ever nurture and develop is *gratitude*. Dr. Mike Murdock says, "Gratitude is the Seed for more."

A great *attitude* will drive you to great accomplishments. Your great attitude will help you...*invoke a blessing on yourself*.

Invoke A Blessing On Yourself.

The Voice That You Listen To Will Determine If You Will Take The Long Path or A Shortcut...

-Yuri I. Tereshchenko

Invoke A Blessing On Yourself.

24

Whose Voice Have You Chosen To Listen To?

The voice you listen to is shaping your life.

One of the most important *differences* in the lives of people is who they have chosen to *listen* to. You do not want *health* advice from an *overweight* person, nor do you pursue *financial* advice from your *broke* friend.

You get to decide if you will go through life in a paddle boat, a canoe, a fishing boat, a jet ski, a speed boat, a barge or whatever other vehicle you may imagine. A mentor in your life will be the *shortcut* to your success; especially one who has *survived* a crisis season.

Mentorship is *learning* through the *pain* of another.

Invoke A Blessing On Yourself.

You may also choose to have a nuclear-powered vessel, with *unlimited* power, for navigating deep waters, without the worry of running out of fuel.

You make the decision on *which* vehicle to use.

"But thou shalt remember the LORD thy God: for it is He that giveth thee power to get wealth, that He may establish His covenant which He swore unto thy fathers, as it is this day," (Deuteronomy 8:18).

God Gave Us Ability And Opportunity.

Our God gave us the *ability*.

You have the *opportunities*; so *look* for them.

Someone said, "If God wants me to be really blessed, He will bless me."

I replied, "If God wants you to have good teeth, He should brush them for you and you can do whatever you want." If you want your hair to look nice all day, God is not going to put hair spray on it. You will have to take care of it yourself.

Dr. Mike Murdock once shared a great example of a conversation he had with an unhealthy, overweight person. They said to him, "God takes care of my body!"

Dr. Murdock replied, "Obviously, He is not doing a good job." We must eat healthy, exercise and take care of our body.

Invoke A Blessing On Yourself.

Many have asked this about The Law of The Seed, "This may work in America, but what about in all the Third World countries?"

The Laws of God Will Work In Any Geographical Location.

Our Father...Jesus...The Holy Spirit...The Faith...and The Word that He gave us are not *restricted* to working in only one geographical location. You can *invoke a blessing on yourself* no matter *where* you are.

The Law of Gravity works the same *everywhere*.

The Law of The Seed also works the same everywhere. If you plant and water your Seed, it will grow and produce fruit. The reason it may *appear* to 'work better' in one area than in another is based on a handful of basic principles and the receptivity of the people to them.

Who do they *listen* to?

How *teachable* are they?

What is their *willingness* to change?

Some people think that God and His Word will *adapt* to their culture; but make no mistake about it. God, The Father, is not American, Ukrainian, British or any other *earthly* nationality. God is God all by Himself.

Invoke A Blessing On Yourself.

He is The Great I AM and biblical principles will work *anywhere* in the world.

I read the story of a young secretary in London, England, who climbed out onto a window ledge, many floors above the ground level. She was threatening to jump, but a young minister leaned over from another window and carried on a conversation with her. She sobbed as she shared about her unhappy life and her feelings of despair.

The minster spoke quietly to her as he tried to assure her that life was *worth* living. For one hour – *sixty golden minutes* – he sought to keep her from jumping.

Eventually, the young woman said, "It's no use. Life just is not worth living." She *jumped* to her death.

If you had the opportunity to speak for one hour to a person who was ready to jump to their death what would you tell them?

Do you have something of value to say to another?

People Don't Care How Much You Know Until They Know How Much You Care.

-Dr. John C. Maxwell

Right out of high school, I started working at a bank. I was earning around $12,000 per year.

Invoke A Blessing On Yourself.

I *expected* increase.

Naturally, as you learn more, you *increase*; but that may not be true for most people. Some people may freeze their pay and lock it in at $20,000 or $30,000 a year, for the rest of their lives, because that is where they are *comfortable*.

Not you...because you are a child of The Most High and you are reading this book.

You are *open-minded*.

You want to *learn*.

You will increase and your wealth will increase.

"Beloved, I wish above all things that thou mayest prosper and be in health, even as thy soul prospereth," (3 John 2).

My income *increased* to $14,000 and then to $16,000, then I got married. My wife and I believed for increase and eventually our earnings *doubled* a couple of times.

What Do You Have On Your Dream Wall?

At one time we believed for a specific truck for our business. My wife and I learned that we needed to have a list and pictures of what we *wanted* on our refrigerator or on a place that we looked at every day.

Invoke A Blessing On Yourself.

Create a dream wall in your home of things that you want to have and do, so you can *visualize* and look at it *every* day; *after* you wake up and *before* you go to bed.

Every time you pass your dream wall, *look* at it.

Visualize what you desire to possess. *Envision* what you want in your Future. Within a year or two after posting the picture on our wall, we got the *perfect* truck for our business.

This faith thing *really* does work.

Whatever level of life you are at...*invoke a blessing on yourself.*

Invoke A Blessing On Yourself.

25

Always Listen To And Listen For The Voice of The Holy Spirit

Listen for The Voice of The Holy Spirit.

Facts and opinions may be important, but 'nothing'…and I repeat 'nothing' can be more important than The Voice of The Holy Spirit. A salesperson may tell you about good tires, a good car, a great house or a great purchase, but…and this is a big but; *listen to The Voice of The Holy Spirit.*

Invoke A Blessing On Yourself.

The Holy Spirit Is The Best Guide On Your Journey To Blessing

-Yuri I. Tereshchenko

Invoke A Blessing On Yourself.

You will *never* go wrong if you attempt to *listen* to The Voice of The Holy Spirit. God will always *reward* you for your *attempt* to listen to The Voice of The Holy Spirit.

If you are not walking with The Holy Spirit, you are not living. Make a decision to be led by The Spirit; and not by people's opinions.

Benefits of Listening To The Voice of The Holy Spirit.

1. Your life may be saved.
2. You will avoid pain.
3. You will avoid loss.
4. You will avoid alimony or bankruptcy.
5. You will move closer to your goals and Assignment.
6. You will be closer to success.
7. You will lead an easier and less complicated life. (It will not necessarily be easy, but it will be easier.)

The Holy Spirit Will Talk To You Through Your Spouse.

When I was buying my BMW, my wife emphasized *restraint* as we making the deal. She wanted to make sure I was not in a hurry, so I could negotiate and get a *better* deal on the car…*and we did.*

Invoke A Blessing On Yourself.

When my wife was ready to purchase an Audi A4, I told her we should *wait,* because the deal was just too perfect. When we called the car dealer the next day, he told us the car had been sold.

We had to begin our search again.

As we searched, we decided to invest a little more and purchase the A6 instead. My wife was glad that we waited. Be *sensitive* to your spouse. The Holy Spirit will often use your spouse to speak to you. One person may be *limited*, but a team of two can be *amazing.* "…one chase a thousand, and two put ten thousand to flight," (Deuteronomy 32:30).

How Would You Like To Always Be At The Right Place At The Right Time?

My goal is to run *every* morning.

One morning, I woke up at 5. It was cold. I really did not want to get out of bed, but I felt I should run that day. When I stepped on the scale, *I knew why.*

As I was running through the parking lot, I saw what I thought was money on the ground. I looked around. There was no one in sight. I had to get on my knees and reach under the cars to collect all the money. Later, when I got home, I counted it. It was about $450 in *cash.*

Invoke A Blessing On Yourself.

Into the savings account it went.

Praise God for such a blessing. It helps to *hear* The Voice of The Holy Spirit. Imagine if you were *always* at the right *place* and the right *time*.

Someone at work asked if I would work late for them on a Wednesday night. After thinking about it, I felt prompted to say, "No." I had been contemplating if I should attend the Wednesday night church service.

That night, at the conclusion of the service, Dr. Mike Murdock gave a $100 bill, and special instructions, to *everyone* present. My wife and I each received $100.

Into the savings account it went.

How would you like to be at the right *place,* at the right *time…every time*?

Oh, if we would *always* listen to The Holy Spirit.

"Simon, Where Is Your Bible?"

Our six year old son had *lost* his Bible.

At his Sunday morning class, they receive a prize for bringing their Bible to class. As my wife and I were about to get him checked in, someone stopped me. They wanted to buy something from the church bookstore.

During church services and events, I serve at The Wisdom Room Bookstore.

The church service had *already* started.

Invoke A Blessing On Yourself.

The bookstore was *closed*.

After checking Simon into his class, we normally go straight into the main service. I could have said, "The Bookstore is closed and the service has started."

Instead, I felt I should attend to this person.

While we were in The Bookstore, we decided to purchase a Bible and Bible cover for our son. When my wife dropped off The Bible at his class, Simon was in tears because he did not have his Bible.

He was so *thankful* that we had bought him a Bible.

See how The Holy Spirit can lead someone to take care of your problem.

It is so important to *obey* The Holy Spirit.

Understanding The Holy Spirit.

The Holy Spirit is a Person.

He is the *Third* Person of The Holy Trinity. The Holy Trinity includes The Father, The Son and The Holy Spirit. The Holy Spirit is *not* a bird...as some pictures may portray.

Moreover, when you pray in The Spirit, you *build* yourself up. "Building up yourselves on your most holy faith, praying in the Holy Ghost," (Jude 1:20).

Invoke A Blessing On Yourself.

There is *another* level that you can attain in praying in The Holy Spirit and that is learning to pray in *warring* tongues...*the strongest level of prayer you can possibly pray.*

One of the reasons you need to habitually use such a prayer language is to *strengthen* you as a Christian, especially if you want to significantly *impact* the spiritual realm.

Steps To Achieving The Highest Level of Prayer...The Warring Tongue.

1. *You Need To Be Filled With The Holy Spirit With Evidence of Speaking In Tongues.*

If you have not yet tapped into your prayer language, one of the last pages of this book contains a prayer for asking The Father to give you that ability. Once you have been filled, with the evidence of speaking in tongues, you can move on to the next step.

2. *Find A Quiet, Private Place Where You Can Be Alone, Without Interruption Or Intimidation.*

Close your eyes. Close your mouth. Without making any sound, pray in the loudest and the strongest tongues you can muster. You will notice that even though you are not making any outward sounds; your tongues...your prayer...*will be coming from your belly.*

Invoke A Blessing On Yourself.

That is the *genuine* prayer in tongues. Jesus said, "…He that believeth on Me, as the scripture hath said, out of his belly shall flow rivers of living water. But this spake He of the Spirit, which they that believe on Him should receive…," (John 7:38-39).

The Holy Spirit Will Direct Your Steps.

Remember when Esther invited the King to dinner.

She initially intended to bring up her concern to the King during the *first* meal, but something was *not* quite right. She then invited the king to a *second* banquet.

"So the king and Haman came to the banquet that Esther had prepared. And the king said unto Esther at the banquet of wine, What is thy petition? and it shall be granted thee: and what is thy request? even to the half of the kingdom it shall be performed.

"Then answered Esther, and said, My petition and my request is; If I have found favour in the sight of the king, and if it please the king to grant my petition, and to perform my request, let the king and Haman come to the banquet that I shall prepare for them, and I will do tomorrow as the king hath said," (Esther 5:5-8).

I believe it is the still, small Voice of The Holy Spirit that that will keep you *out* of trouble and *in* the will and blessing of God.

Invoke A Blessing On Yourself.

Listening to The Voice of The Holy Spirit and praying in the Spirit will help you on your journey as you...*invoke a blessing on yourself.*

Invoke A Blessing On Yourself.

You May Want To Invoke Blessing On Others, But Ultimately Your Goal Is To Invoke A Blessing On Yourself First. That Will Be A Great Accomplishment, Because If You Can Invoke A Blessing On Yourself It Has A Ripple Effect.

-Yuri I. Tereshchenko

Invoke A Blessing On Yourself.

26

Why Job Got What He Really, Really Did Not Want?

Job was a man God *respected*

We read in The Bible, "There was a man in the land of Uz, whose name was Job; and that man was perfect and upright, and one that feared God, and eschewed evil," (Job 1:1).

Job had seven sons and three daughters. Job was the *greatest* of all men of the East and God's hand of protection was over him. Satan came before The Lord and after their conversation, killed Job's children and destroyed Job's wealth. (See Job 1.)

One of the reasons Job had to go through such a terrible trial was because of his own *thoughts*. "For the

Invoke A Blessing On Yourself.

thing which I greatly feared is come upon me and that which I was afraid of is come unto me," (Job 3:35).

What was it that Job feared? "And his sons went and feasted in their houses, everyone his day; and sent and called for their three sisters to eat and to drink with them. And it was so, when the days of their feasting were gone about, that Job sent and sanctified them, and rose up early in the morning, and offered burnt offerings according to the number of them all: for Job said, It may be that my sons have sinned, and cursed God in their hearts. Thus did Job continually," (Job 1:4-5).

> Invoke A Blessing On Yourself And Everything That Surrounds You, Everything That You Touch, And Everything That You Influence.
>
> -Yuri I. Tereshchenko

There is a thin line between acting in *Honor*...and doing something because of *fear, unbelief* or *distrust*.

Let me elaborate. When I get up early in the morning, the *first* thing I do is brush my teeth. Not because I am afraid that they will fall out if I do not take care of them, but because I want to *prevent* anything bad from happening.

Invoke A Blessing On Yourself.

The *second* thing I do is pray to The Father in The Name of Jesus. I do not pray because I am afraid something bad is going to happen, even though it could. When I pray, I thank The Father for everything I *have* and I thank Him for everything He is *about* to give me, because I believe I *already* have it.

I thank Him for daily protection and blessing on my family, friends, and others. I thank God for The Blood of Jesus that covers us and for angelic protection over us.

I invoke a blessing on myself, my family and everything that *surrounds* me…everything that I *touch* and everyone that I *influence*.

Why Should You Invoke The Blessing On Yourself?

I do not do all this praying and invoking because I am afraid. I do it in advance to *prevent* anything negative from even germinating. I take *authority* over my life and my Future because I am a spirit living in a human body.

God made us this way. Everything happens first in the spirit world *before* it happens in the natural.

That is what I believe Job did *not* know.

Job also rose up early in the morning, just like I do, but in his spirit he had ingrained the following words, "It may be that my sons have sinned, and cursed God in their hearts. Thus I will offer burnt offering daily."

Invoke A Blessing On Yourself.

Let me give you a different scenario so you can clearly understand what I am attempting to convey here.

4 Ways People Process Information.

1. When You Are Unconsciously Incompetent You Do Not Know What You Do Not Know. An example would be a child who does not know *how* to ride a bike, or how to drive a car...until someone teaches them.

It is possible for them to discover new things for themselves. They just do not know what they do not know. Even as an adult there are many things you may not know. What you do not have...*you do not know how to receive.*

2. When You Are Consciously Incompetent You Discover Information You Know You Did Not Know Before. That is when you realize that you are *incompetent.* You did not know *how* to drive a car until you observed, practiced and learned.

3. When You Are Unconsciously Competent You Function On Autopilot. You are capable of tying the laces on your shoes, driving your car or riding your bike without much thought.

As you drive on the same road to work every day, you may talk on your cell phone the *entire* drive, because you *know* the road. Suddenly, you find yourself pulling

Invoke A Blessing On Yourself.

into the parking lot at your office. You did not even notice how many cars there were, because you were preoccupied with your important phone conversation.

  4. When You Are Consciously Competent, You Know That You Know And You Are Confident of It. For example, you know that you know how to do drive a car, you are confident driving your car, and it becomes easier and easier.

  When you act in Honor, consciously and competently, you will...*invoke a blessing on yourself.*

Invoke A Blessing On Yourself.

I Will Study And Prepare And My Opportunity Will Come.

—Abraham Lincoln.

Invoke A Blessing On Yourself.

27

You Are The Commander of Your Destiny, The Master of Your Ship

Your thinking *determines* the outcome of your life.

It is imperative that you *feed* your Mind with the right information. *Read* the right books. *Listen* to good Bible based teaching. If you are around negative people, or are constantly watching or listening to the news, you will live in fear. I am not speaking against watching the news, but there must be a *balance*.

You *decide* your balance. It will depend on how much positive, uplifting information versus negative information you absorb.

Invoke A Blessing On Yourself.

You may think this is a tall order or whether it is really possible, but as you read this book and learn these principles, you will be reminded of the verse in Mark 10:27, "with God all things are possible."

> You Cannot Have A Great Life Unless You Have A Pure Life; You Cannot Have A Pure Life Unless You Have A Pure Mind; You Cannot Have A Pure Mind Unless You Wash It Daily With The Word of God.
>
> -Dr. Mike Murdock

Some of the concepts in this book may sound *farfetched*, but you will be reminded by The Holy Spirit that *nothing* is impossible to him who believes.

Most people have the goal of having peace, harmony and happiness. You will need to *monitor* your thoughts in order to *experience* these feelings. Your thoughts cause your feelings and your feelings cause your thoughts. The process is cyclic; thoughts then feelings, feelings then thoughts, and so on and so forth.

You tend to produce *more* of whatever you are *focused* on, so you might as well work on having good thoughts to maintain good feelings, which will produce more good thoughts and more good feelings.

When you feel *good,* you will feel *blessed* and *able*.

Invoke A Blessing On Yourself.

You will be *empowered* to accomplish *great* things; and that will cause *more* blessings to flow into your life.

YOU have the power to *create* a pleasant experience, or chaos and disorder, on a daily basis.

YOU are in control, *not God.*

Is God Really In Control...?

God is *not* in control of your life, YOU are.

God has *predestined* the consequences of your decisions. If you think this is heresy, let me point out several examples:

1. If God is in control, why are children born *crippled*?
2. If God is in control, why are children *abused*?
3. If God is in control, why do children go to bed *hungry*?
4. If God is in control, why is the world in such a *mess*?
5. If God is in control, why are women *raped*?
6. If God is in control, why isn't everyone *saved*?
7. If God is in control, why do so many people commit *suicide*?
8. If God is in control, why do most people *suffer* on earth?
9. If God is in control, why do people get *sick* and *die*?
10. If God is in control, why do most people live in *sin*?

Invoke A Blessing On Yourself.

You are in control of your mouth, your decisions and indecisions, your actions, reactions and non actions.

You are in control of your *daily* activities.

You Control Your Life.

You control or restrict your income.

Your decisions will affect your rewards in life.

God has already predestined the consequences of your decisions. Your Future may be preordained, but it is *controlled* by your decisions.

You may be the one who caused an automobile accident by attracting it to you. When you are upset and unfocused behind the wheel, you attract disorder. Your decisions in turn created chain reactions.

Your decisions will *always* decide your Future.

This great book, *Invoke A Blessing On Yourself*, will help you understand that God has already given you everything you *need*. You must learn how to use what has been made available to you.

You will need to learn how to command your destiny and captain your own ship.

One sentence from this book may not necessarily deliver you and lead you out of your situation *instantly*. Read this book through several times. Read it carefully to

Invoke A Blessing On Yourself.

get the *whole* picture of what you have to do. There are hidden truths you will gain after re-reading this book.
    I recommend you read other great books as well.
    Becoming a magnet for information will...*invoke a blessing on yourself.*

Invoke A Blessing On Yourself.

Worrying Is Planning To Fail, Because You Concentrate On The Problem And Not The Solution.

-Yuri I. Tereshchenko

Invoke A Blessing On Yourself.

28

Have You Ever Lost What You Had Already Gained?

Anything gained can be *lost*.

Some people make tremendous accomplishments in their careers and businesses. In the process, they accumulate *luxury* items and get accustomed to *plush* lifestyles.

In attempting to *protect* their luxurious lifestyle, they may be asking, "What do I need to do to avoid losing what I have?" If their Minds are preoccupied with potential loss, their mental pictures will be dominated by losing...*which means they will eventually experience losses.*

Several close friends of mine started a *great* business. Shortly afterwards, they engaged in conversations with people who convinced them that they

Invoke A Blessing On Yourself.

risked *losing* everything they owned because it was going to be difficult for them to run their operations profitably in this economy.

Negative people will *always* pour cold water on your fire.

What Are You Speaking Over Your Environment?

From that day forward, instead of declaring that their business would prosper, they constantly discussed the negative results and poor performance. "If our business fails we may lose our cars and our house. If we cannot keep this business going, everything we have worked so hard for will be lost."

Eventually, their business started to fail because that was what they had been *declaring*. "Any day now they will be knocking on our door and kicking us out of our own house."

After internalizing the negative remarks, they started to *doubt* that their business could succeed.

They wanted attention and sympathy from others, so they spoke unbelief, doubt and negativity. They would say to each other, "Can you believe that we have invested everything we had saved up and we are now so close to losing it all?"

Invoke A Blessing On Yourself.

The thought of losing *everything* you have saved up for retirement can put anyone in depression. Unfortunately, they chose to spend all their time *meditating* on and *discussing* their failure...*so it happened.*

When You Think About Something Most of The Time...You Will Get It.

Some *think* about, *talk* about, and *pray* against loss.

If you pray against loss your Mind announces, "Loss...loss...loss." Focus your prayers instead on: Favor, Blessing, Prosperity, Sales, Abundance and Increase.

My friends chose to concentrate on their own loss.

They *caused* their own failure; initially with their *thoughts*...and then later by their *words*.

Most of their friends were also 'concerned' about them, so they also *thought* and *talked* about loss; in *agreement* with them as well as on their *behalf*.

Be careful with whom you share your personal issues. Most people have negative tendencies. It is *natural* for them to speak negatively. It takes conscious effort to speak *positive* things.

Everything, to the last word, happened.

They went out of business. They lost almost everything they had. They had no clue they were the

Invoke A Blessing On Yourself.

cause of it. Many around them contributed to the failure with their *negative* words and *misdirected* prayers.

What you *think*, you will *believe*.

What you believe, you will eventually *speak*.

In time, what you speak will come to pass in your life, because you *attracted* it.

With your thinking, you can...*invoke a blessing on yourself.*

29

Invoke A Blessing Or A Curse...

Your decisions will decide what you attract.

You have three options. You can invoke a *blessing*, you can invoke *nothing* or you can invoke a *curse*. When you sow a Seed into good ground, it will bring you a Harvest. When you sow nothing, you will receive a Harvest of *nothing*. When you sow discord, negativity or live in sin, you will reap a *curse*.

That is right; you can sow for a curse.

No one *wants* a curse. That is why The Bible warns, "My people are destroyed for lack of knowledge:

Invoke A Blessing On Yourself.

*I Don't Invoke Blessings On Myself To Live,
But I Live To Invoke A Blessing Upon Myself*
　　　　-Yuri I. Tereshchenko

Invoke A Blessing On Yourself.

because thou hast rejected knowledge, I will also reject thee, that thou shalt be no priest to Me: seeing thou hast forgotten the law of thy God, I will also forget thy children," (Hosea 4:6).

Learning Honor and Respect will make your life so much easier, because, in the process, you will learn to master everything else. Some people *expect* bad things to happen because they think that is the *normal* way to live. They incorrectly think they are doing God's will because of the devil's attacks against them; but not so.

You can invoke your Future upon yourself.

Do it and take charge of your life.

You Are The Product of Your Thoughts.

"The weapons of our warfare are not carnal, but mighty through God to the pulling down of strong holds; Casting down imaginations, and every high thing that exalteth itself against the knowledge of God, and bringing into captivity every thought to the obedience of Christ," (2 Corinthians 10:4-5).

Everything you have, you *created* with your thoughts. It is not necessarily what you *did*, but what you *thought* that created what you have. If there is something you really, really want or do not want, you will get it.

What you *keep* thinking about is what you will *get*.

Invoke A Blessing On Yourself.

> If You Are Satisfied With Your Sowing You Should Be Satisfied With Your Harvest.
>
> If You Are Satisfied With What You Believe, You Should Be Satisfied With What You Have.
>
> -Dr. Mike Murdock

If what you have been thinking does not bring you joy, it is not *worth* the trouble.

A Simple Formula For Controlling Your Thoughts.

How do you *control* your thoughts?

How do you *streamline* your thinking to attract *what* you want? It helps to be a *positive* person. Once you make a deliberate decision to be more positive, you will catch yourself every time you think negative thoughts or say negative words. If you keep working at it, you will *eventually* become better at maintaining positive thinking.

Keep doing it over and over again until you *naturally* lean toward positive thoughts and positive words. Positive thinking will become a *subconscious* act, like tying your shoes.

Invoke A Blessing On Yourself.

Doing something over and over again creates energy pathways in the brain that we call a *habit*.

An interesting story is found in Daniel 1:8. "Daniel purposed in his heart that he would not defile himself with the portion of the king's meat, or with the wine which he drank: therefore he requested of the prince of the eunuchs that he might not defile himself," (Daniel 1:8 NKJV).

God had brought Daniel favor. It is said of Daniel that he had an excellent spirit, wisdom, knowledge, and understanding to interpret dreams, clarify riddles, and solve knotty problems. (See Daniel 5:12 AMP).

After Daniel interpreted the king's dream, the king elevated Daniel to be above all the presidents and satraps. (See Daniel 6:3, AMP.)

Right Thoughts Will Lead You Toward Blessing.

Recently, I saw an interesting illustration of two men who were both planting trees in the heat of the day.

The *first* man who was planting a tree wore an orange jump suit. In the background, there was a man on a horse holding a shotgun.

The *second* man who was planting a tree was wearing shorts and a t-shirt. His wife, a young, beautiful woman, stood in the background with an ice cold drink.

Invoke A Blessing On Yourself.

Two men. Doing exactly the *same* thing.

Yet, in two *different* environments...with two different *reasons* for doing what they did...and living two different *lifestyles*.

The Bible directs us toward the "renewing of our minds." (See Romans 12:2).

Make sure you choose the *right* environment.

Only there can you...*invoke the blessing on yourself.*

Invoke A Blessing On Yourself.

30

The Blessing Will Reside In Your Thoughts...And In Your Mind

Your Mind is your garden.

Take good care of your garden. Feed it with high-quality, positive information. My Mind is *more* important than my wife and children, because if my Mind is healthy I can take good care of my family...

In Romans 12:2, we read, "be not conformed to this world: but be ye transformed by the renewing of your mind, that ye may prove what is that good, and acceptable, and perfect, will of God."

When we listen to worldly views and worldly programming we *store* that information. That information can *create* phobias. These worldly ideas can *mold* your

Invoke A Blessing On Yourself.

Behavior Is The Accurate Unerring Interpreter of Hidden Thoughts, Unknown Feelings And Opinions.

-Dr. Mike Murdock

Invoke A Blessing On Yourself.

thoughts; and if you are not well-versed scripturally, they *will* control you negatively.

By going to church, fellowshipping with other believers and listening to The Word of God, our Mind will get *renewed*. When we read great books, our Mind conforms to the ideas presented.

Often, the world thinks Christians are crazy to think and believe God's Word, but the reality is those who do *not* believe The Word of God are *crazy*.

The worlds *began* with The Word of God, they now *exist* by The Word of God, and they will *end* only by The Word of God. "Through faith we understand that the worlds were framed by the word of God, so that things which are seen were not made of things which do appear," (Hebrews 11:3).

> The Battle of Life Is For Your Mind; The Battle of The Mind Is For Focus.
>
> -Dr. Mike Murdock

I know some people that keep saying, "I have always been self employed, so I am not good at submitting to a boss, being an employee; so I keep losing jobs." Then they also say: "I do not know how to run my

Invoke A Blessing On Yourself.

own business." In this case, the consequence of speaking wrong words is continuous financial *failure*.

Decide what you are going to do. Speak it and bring it to pass, otherwise you will keep failing financially.

The Power of Your Mind.

Your Mind is very sophisticated.

One reputable physician estimated that 75% of people that visit doctors are suffering from *imaginary* illnesses. If a person strongly *believes* they have a certain sickness, their body may *manifest* the physical symptoms of the actual disease.

Your Mind is very powerful.

With your Mind, you can *build* or *destroy*. The same applies to a hex or a spell. If you believe you can be hexed, then according to your faith, you will have what you believe. "For the thing which I greatly feared is come upon me, and that which I was afraid of is come unto me," (Job 3:25).

I believe I am covered by The Blood of Jesus. No hex or spell can *penetrate* the hedge of protection over me or my house.

There is strong evidence to suggest that most sicknesses and diseases start in your Mind. That is why I

Invoke A Blessing On Yourself.

wrote this book so you can...*invoke a BLESSING on yourself* instead.

Your blessing is based on what you *think* about *most* of the time. It comes to pass when you believe it to be so and when you say that you have it as though you do. Speak it with faith. Make a decision to feel good about receiving your Blessing.

The Holy Spirit will *confirm* if it is of God.

Invoke A Blessing On Yourself.

An Eagle Protégé Will Require An Eagle Mentor.

-Yuri I. Tereshchenko

Invoke A Blessing On Yourself.

31

Do Not Peck Like A Chicken...Soar Like An Eagle

Eagles and chickens experience *different* lifestyles.

The first time I heard this example was from Dr. Mike Murdock. The eagle and the chicken are comfortable in two completely different environments.

The conversation of a chicken around the barn will be different from that of the eagle that soars *high* above the mountains. People have a choice. They would rather soar like an eagle, but most are not willing to pay the price necessary to live there.

You will have to pay a price to become a person of *value*. The more valuable you are the more compensation you will *attract*.

Invoke A Blessing On Yourself.

Eagles are *leaders*.

An eagle does not fly in a pack because it does not *require* motivation. Leaders are *self-motivated* individuals. When you feel down and discouraged or unmotivated take walks...get some fresh air. A walk can *clear* your Mind and help you get *refocused*.

> Eagles And Chickens Have Different Conversations.
>
> -Dr. Mike Murdock

As you walk through the park, or in a relaxing outdoor environment, you will realize that the *possibilities* in the world are so much *bigger* than the limitations of your situation or problem. As you walk, listen to some *motivational* or *uplifting* music.

Praying in tongues while you walk will help immensely. Do not depend on your understanding, but *trust* The Holy Spirit. If you are unable to discern the problem, you will not be able to *correct* it. The Holy Spirit will *reveal* what you need to do *next*.

Leaders are readers, because they must *consistently* learn. Invest time to grow and learn. Everyone considers themselves to be *busy*. The billionaire is busy because he has to *manage* his billion dollar business. The guy on

Invoke A Blessing On Yourself.

welfare is busy too. It is not how many hours you put in, but what you put *into* your hours.

What Picture Do You Have of Yourself?

You become who you *think* you are.

If you think you are *beaten*, you are. If you think you cannot *dare* to achieve anything, you will not. If you think you cannot win, you will never overcome. If you think you will lose, then you have *already* lost. It is all in your Mind. If you think you are outclassed, you are.

Become *sure* of yourself. Develop *confidence* in your ability. Become the kind of person who envisions *victory* and *success*. Network with the right people who can help support your growth. Make sure you have high quality mentors in your life.

Be wary of *wrong* relationships.

Listening is the most important part of communication. Evaluate what people say. Listen to what is *said* and what is left *unsaid*. When you listen *intently* you will be able to pick up important information that pertains to your relationship with that person. Be careful of what you say.

Speak *life*, not death.

Never say, "I am going to try."

Invoke A Blessing On Yourself.

'Try' means you may or may not do it. It is hard to have a relationship with a *wavering* person. Your Mind sees in pictures, so 'try' tells your Mind there is no commitment.

Instead, *emphatically* say, "I will do it

Never say, "That blows my Mind."

It may seem a small thing, but it is *imperative* that you stop invoking negativity on yourself. Never say what you do not want. Speaking negatively attracts miserable events into your life. Talking negative is like attracting an ad like this into your life, "For Sale: Parachute. Only used once, never opened, has a small stain."

The spiritual world around you will *deliver* what you expect and speak over your life. Direct your conversation to…*invoke a blessing on yourself.*

Invoke A Blessing On Yourself.

32

Nurture And Develop Worthwhile Relationships

Your relationships *affect* your success.

Your income can be predicted by taking the sum of what your five *closest* friends earn right now, dividing it by 5; and the result is approximately what you will be earning in 5 years. If you do not like the result, you may have to find some *new* friends.

Success *breeds* success.

Association with successful people will *motivate* you to succeed. Observing, watching, and listening to the successful will *birth* new ideas.

I am not telling you who to be, or who not to be friends with, I simply want to show you what your friendships will produce for you.

Invoke A Blessing On Yourself.

*Be Slow In Choosing A Friend,
Slower In Changing Him.*

-Benjamin Franklin

Invoke A Blessing On Yourself.

Samson's decisions and involvement with Delilah initially cost him his eyesight, then *later* his life. (See Judges 16.)

Every Friendship Has A Cost And A Reward.

Every friendship has a *price*.

Your children may hear a relative saying, "I am sick with this and aggravated with that. I have no control over this outcome." On the other hand, you may have been training your children never to say what they do not want, but to speak into existence what they desire.

When they encounter negative influences from such acquaintances, you will pay the price for training that was not implemented because of a *conflicting* role model. You must identify the differences in your relationships. The person you trust may trust someone you never will. Identify that *third* relationship.

You will not last in a relationship that *drains* you.

There are times you may have to refrain from certain associations. You have to *protect* good relationships, but do not be overly aggressive in your approach. You will have different *levels* of relationships.

Never take advantage of a friendship that has been extended to you by opening the door *wider* than it was opened for you. If you are offered a gift, do not demand

Invoke A Blessing On Yourself.

for a *second* one. "When thou sittest to eat with a ruler, consider diligently what is before thee: And put a knife to thy throat, if thou be a man given to appetite," (Proverbs 23:1-2).

If you are invited into their *private* world, never stay too *long*. "Withdraw thy foot from thy neighbour's house; lest he be weary of thee, and so hate thee," (Proverbs 25:17).

Never become too *familiar* with your friends and acquaintances. Familiarity can turn into *disrespect*.

Honor is a Seed for *long* relationships.

A Tribute To Friendship

I love you not only for what you are, but for what I am when I am with you;

I love you not only for what you have made of yourself, but for what you are making of me;

I love you not for closing your ears to the discords in me, but for adding to the music in me by worshipful listening;

You have done it without a touch, without a word, without a sign. You have done it just by being yourself. Perhaps that is what being a friend means, after all.

-Author Unknown.

Invoke A Blessing On Yourself.

    Relationships are investments of time and money, so *analyze* your relationships. An *old* friend is better than two *new* ones. Your relationships should be such that they help *invoke a blessing* for all involved.

Invoke A Blessing On Yourself.

Who Can Find A Virtuous Woman? For Her Price Is Far Above Rubies.

-Proverbs 31:10

Invoke A Blessing On Yourself.

33

The Proverbs 31 Woman

The Proverbs 31 Woman is a *rare* woman.

The Proverbs 31 Woman is a great example of the *foundation* for invoking a blessing on yourself. As you read Proverbs 31, you cannot help but notice several extremely important, uncommon qualities that are needed to become a successful, quality woman.

A woman of such quality may be difficult to locate, but she is not impossible to find.

I will tell you a family *secret*.

As far as I am concerned, there are two young ladies that I know of, who are being raised up right now. I am sure there may be many, many more, but I would like to tell you about one that is already a part of my life

Invoke A Blessing On Yourself.

and another one that will be a part of my family in about fifteen to twenty years.

One I know personally, our daughter, Deonna.

The other one will be the wife for our son, Simon.

We do not know her yet, but she will be a *quality* woman. *My wife and I will make sure of it!*

> You Don't Just Give A $10,000 Violin To A 500 lb. Gorilla To Play With...
>
> -Yuri I. Tereshchenko

Only an uncommon man can *attract* this uncommon lady. I remember having a conversation with a very nice couple from our church, The Wisdom Center. While preaching, our senior pastor, Dr. Mike Murdock, had strongly suggested that before you give your daughter away, you should check her future husband's credit history, as well as his checking and savings accounts.

The man we were talking to told us it would have been hard for him to *qualify* for his wife, because he did not have a lot of money when they first met. My wife glanced at me. Since I was in a listening mode, I just smiled and nodded.

Invoke A Blessing On Yourself.

Later, I revisited the conversation. During my quiet time, I *ponder* things I have heard or seen, to process and extract information from *each* experience.

I quietly evaluated my friend's statement.

When our daughter was a baby, she did not sleep well. We had to consistently change her diaper. (Notice I did not say *only* one of us, because I am a full time father. When I am at home, I am *actively* involved with what goes on...*I am no couch potato!*)

By the time our daughter is grown up, my wife and I would have spent sleepless nights raising her. We would have invested time and money raising our children in a high *quality* environment; making *sacrifices* so we can build a great Future for them.

I would be hesitant to release my daughter's hand in marriage to a man who has been *unable* to have a measure of success as a *single* man. If he cannot succeed as a single man, how will he succeed as a *married* one?

The Proverbs 31 Woman Is Not For Sale.

A high quality woman cannot be bought, she is not for sale. "Her price is far above rubies," (Proverbs 31:10).

She knows her *value*.

She knows her *Difference* from others.

Invoke A Blessing On Yourself.

The Proverbs 31 Woman requires *pursuit*. She is financially competent and sound. She is not short on cash. She is comfortable with or without money. She does not run to the mall every time she is given a $100 bill. She understands business. She is *strategic* and *confident*. If her husband is *unable* to produce enough money to support the family, she will work to *assist* him.

She brings more value to the marriage than the money they have. She brings more significance and satisfaction to her husband than his business can.

Her man can *depend* on her. They work harmoniously *together*. He finds *peace* in her arms. He will always pursue her because all others pale in comparison to her. He is proud of her and proud to be *with* her every chance he gets.

The Proverbs 31 Woman Is Trustworthy.

Everything may collapse around him, but she is his world. "The heart of her husband doth safely trust in her, so that he shall have no need of spoil," (Proverbs 31:11).

Every man trusts a woman.

The *first* woman he trusts is *usually* his mother.

When he leaves his mother and father, and cleaves to his wife, that trust will then be *transferred* to his wife forever. "And said, For this cause shall a man leave father

Invoke A Blessing On Yourself.

and mother, and shall cleave to his wife: and they twain shall be one flesh?" (Matthew 19:5).

Her husband can trust her without *reserve*.

He can *trust* her with his strengths and weaknesses, with money and secrets. He can *confide* in her his memories and fears. He has *confidence* in her fidelity. He can trust her with his friends and he can trust her in his absence.

She is not a burden to him. She does not create trouble for him by her actions. She is never a distraction or an embarrassment to him. She will not slow him down nor stifle the greatness within him. She will never discourage or pull him down; but will *protect* and *encourage* him.

The Proverbs 31 woman is a *multiplier* of good things and experiences in her husband's life. "She will do him good and not evil all the days of her life," (Proverbs 31:12).

She is not lazy. She is not a busybody. She does not sit around the house all day watching soaps on T.V., and daydreaming how she can have a 'life' like the people on the screen.

Her destiny is in her hands. Instead of sitting around imagining and dreaming, she brings her dreams to pass. She *loves* to work. "She seeketh wool, and flax, and worketh willingly with her hands," (Proverbs 31:13).

Invoke A Blessing On Yourself.

The Proverbs 31 Woman Is Willing.

"Willingly" is such a powerful word for me.

Willingly means you do not have to beg, plead, beseech or implore. She notices that something needs to be done and she willingly and happily does it. It brings such pleasure and amazement to me when I see someone that does a job willingly.

The Encyclopedia of 15,000 Illustrations, by Paul Lee Tan, lists seven reasons *why* most women buy things.
1. Her husband says she *cannot* have it.
2. It will make her *look* thin.
3. It comes from *Paris*.
4. The neighbors *cannot* afford it.
5. *Nobody* has one.
6. *Everybody* has one.
7. It is *different*.

The Proverbs 31 Woman Is Financially Savvy.

The Proverbs 31 Woman is a shopper.

She is not a spendthrift, and does not spend money foolishly. She has checking and savings accounts fat with cash.

Invoke A Blessing On Yourself.

She is an *investor*. She invests in products and services that either *save* her money or *make* her money. Unfortunately, many women frivolously spend money on the next gadget or fashion accessory.

The Proverbs 31 Woman *understands* and *studies* money. She carefully observes the right and wrong ways of handling her finances. She has been trained to be careful with money. She is skilled at negotiating for and getting the best possible deals and value.

"They Were On Sale...!"

A young lady I know has a lot of clothes in her closet that still have tags on them. She *never* wears them.

She bought them because they were on *sale*.

It reminds me of a story I read of lady from Spain.

She saved her earnings for twelve years until she finally had enough to pay for her heart's desire – a sailboat. She had the boat put in her backyard, because she was *terrified* of the water.

Many women either squander or hoard their money, because they want to make a show of what they have. However, the Proverbs 31 Woman earns and sows her money. She is *comfortable* managing money.

Over the years, I have worked in several banks. I have seen how much money people *make* and *save*. I saw

Invoke A Blessing On Yourself.

millions of dollars on a daily basis, but I knew that the money was not mine to *take*. I was trained to show respect, to never take what did not belong to me. I have chosen to live by those rules because I value my *freedom*.

The Proverbs 31 woman is *skilled* in handling finances. Access to money does not *tempt* or *corrupt* her. She is *comfortable* with what she earns. She demonstrates respect for others by being a person of honesty and integrity. She enjoys work. She does not grumble or complain about long hours.

I personally enjoy being productive.

I cannot just sit idle around the house. Some people can, I cannot. I *have* to be productive. I have to learn, do and accomplish. I have to be *active*, so I rarely get bored. As I grew up, I was trained to work diligently and consistently.

Many people have learnt to *appear* busy and *act* as if they are working, yet they are not.

The Proverbs 31 Woman Is Worker.

The Proverbs 31 Woman does not protest against going the *extra* mile to get what is needed for her family.

She is like a ship...*constantly in movement*. "She is like the merchants' ships; she bringeth her food from afar," (Proverbs 31:14).

Invoke A Blessing On Yourself.

She habitually rises *early*. "She riseth also while it is yet night...," (Proverbs 31:15).

Some people require more sleep than others.

I am amazed when someone tells me there are not enough hours in a day and later on discloses they *sleep* ten to twelve hours a day. Only a few people can sleep that many hours and still be productive.

If you cannot demonstrate productivity with just a few hours of work a day, please consider the following quote, "Insanity is when a person keeps doing the same thing over and over again and expects to see different results."

The Proverbs 31 Woman Is Productive.

Time management is of the essence if you want to be productive. The Proverbs 31 Woman is *focused*, her time is *precious*. She plans her day and she gets results, because she can *manage* her schedule. She is good at business. "She considereth a field, and buyeth it: with the fruit of her hands she planteth a vineyard," (Proverbs 31:16).

She is *intelligent* and *smart*.
She is *well-versed* in business.
She is *educated* and well *read*.
She *understands* The Laws of Increase.

Invoke A Blessing On Yourself.

She *strives* for knowledge and success.

She does not make hasty decisions, she makes *right* decisions. She will ask the questions necessary to make *intelligent* decisions.

She will not act impulsively.

She is thorough, cautious and patient.

To get good, profitable deals in business, you have to be knowledgeable of the market and the products. To flourish in your business, or your career, you must possess, nurture and develop the success qualities described above.

The Proverbs 31 Woman Takes Care of Her Health.

She is physically fit. She eats the right foods. She exercises. She is healthy and strong. A doctor stated that people who are fit physically do not fall into depression. If you feel well, you will do well; but if you do not your productivity will be affected.

"She girdeth her loins with strength, and strengtheneth her arms. She perceiveth that her merchandise is good: her candle goeth not out by night," (Proverbs 31:17-18).

The Proverbs 31 woman may be as *active* as a merchant's ship, but she does not *look* like one!

Invoke A Blessing On Yourself.

She is not in a hurry to go to bed every night. She completes the projects she starts and attends to her responsibilities. She does not sleep 12 hours a day. She stays up late and wakes up early, because her time is very *valuable*.

"She layeth her hands to the spindle, and her hands hold the distaff. She stretcheth out her hand to the poor; yea, she reacheth forth her hands to the needy," (Proverbs 31:19-20).

She is diligent, observant and compassionate for she *reaches* out to the poor. She has stability in her life because she can relate to the *high* class, the *middle* class and even the *poor*.

The Proverbs 31 Woman Is Adaptable.

"She is not afraid of the snow for her household: for all her household are clothed with scarlet. She maketh herself coverings of tapestry; her clothing is silk and purple. Her husband is known in the gates, when he sitteth among the elders of the land. She maketh fine linen, and selleth it; and delivereth girdles unto the merchant. Strength and honour are her clothing; and she shall rejoice in time to come," (Proverbs 31:21-25).

She is prepared for any *season* or *change* in her personal life and in the life of her family.

Invoke A Blessing On Yourself.

> She has good taste.
> She dresses for success.
> She takes good care of herself and her husband.

Her husband is known and *respected* in the community. She is a good sales person and negotiator. She is self-confident and secure. Her self-confidence generates her inner peace. She looks forward to her Future, because she has invested plenty of time *preparing* for it.

The Proverbs 31 Woman Is Honorable With Her Words.

"She openeth her mouth with wisdom; and in her tongue is the law of kindness. She looketh well to the ways of her household, and eateth not the bread of idleness. Her children arise up, and call her blessed; her husband also, and he praiseth her. Many daughters have done virtuously, but thou excellest them all. Favour is deceitful, and beauty is vain: but a woman that feareth the Lord, she shall be praised. Give her of the fruit of her hands; and let her own works praise her in the gates," (Proverbs 31:26-31).

Her words have *power*. She is skillful with her conversation. She is a learned and educated woman, so she uses her words wisely and appropriately.

Her words are *always* kind.

Invoke A Blessing On Yourself.

She *finishes* what she starts. Her children enjoy her, and her husband is proud of her. She fears The Lord and cannot be compared to or rivaled by another.

Your background does not matter.

As you follow the Proverbs 31 principles, you will succeed; and as you succeed, your children will model their lives *after* you. If you raise your children to such a level of discipline, their success is *guaranteed*.

When you are old, they will take good care of you.

The Proverbs 31 woman knows how to…*invoke a blessing on herself.*

Invoke A Blessing On Yourself.

Last Chapter of The Book, But New Chapter In Your Life.

-Yuri I. Tereshchenko

Invoke A Blessing On Yourself.

34

In Conclusion…

We have covered a lot of ground in this book.

Blessing and success is not measured by what you have. Success is measured by who you are becoming.

Things can be *lost* or taken away.

Zig Ziglar shared a story about some young men who worked at a gas station. The turnover rate at the gas station was high, probably because the pay was low. The agreement between the owner and the workers was they would provide very *high* quality service for really *low* pay. The people that came to get gas would hire them out because they were *impressed* with the quality of service.

The plan was pure genius, because these young men learned work ethics. After they were hired out, they

Invoke A Blessing On Yourself.

would still come *back* to this gas station because of the high quality service.

When patrons of the gas station became successful they would hire the young men working at the gas station, because they knew the owner was training these young men to become *quality* employees.

Invoke A Blessing On Yourself.

Invoke Salvation On Yourself

Prayer To Accept Jesus As Your Savior

Will you accept Jesus as your personal Savior today?
The Bible says, "That if thou shalt confess with thy mouth the Lord Jesus, and shalt believe in thine heart that God hath raised Him from the dead, thou shalt be saved," (Romans 10:9)
Pray this prayer from your heart today!
"Dear Jesus, I believe that You died for me and rose again on the third day. I confess I am a sinner. I need Your love and forgiveness. Come into my heart. Forgive my sins. I receive Your eternal life. Confirm Your love by giving me peace, joy and supernatural love for others. In Jesus' Name, Amen."

Invoke A Blessing On Yourself.

Prayer To Receive The Gift of The Holy Spirit

This Gift is available to *every* believer.

This may be a *new* revelation to you, so I will explain it in detail. After receiving Jesus as your Savior, you have the opportunity to receive The Gift of The Holy Spirit with the evidence of "speaking in other tongues." (See Acts 2:4.)

Accepting Jesus Is The First Step In The Process.

You must *first* receive Jesus as your Savior to receive The Gift of The Holy Spirit. "Jesus saith unto him, I am the Way, the Truth, and the Life: no man cometh unto the Father, but by Me," (John 14:6).

You do not have to *beg* God to give you the empowering of His Spirit. As a born again believer, you *invite* The Holy Spirit to have complete access to your life. After you have prayed the following prayer, move your lips and what may seem as "strange words" will begin to fill your mouth.

Do not try to *understand* them with your Mind.

Invoke A Blessing On Yourself.

Your Mind may try to resist this, for you will be speaking words foreign to your natural thinking.

Try speaking in the spirit in other tongues *before* you have prayed. It does not work, does it? You do not really know what to say, so you definitely know it is not your Mind that made it up. "Wherefore let him that speaketh in an unknown tongue pray that he may interpret. For if I pray in an unknown tongue, my spirit prayeth, but my understanding is unfruitful," (1 Corinthians 14:13-14).

Fear Not...

Do not be afraid of receiving something of the devil. Before you received Jesus, you were never taught you could worship the devil with another tongue.

When people sit in bars, do they speak to each other in tongues? *No.* Instead, they spontaneously *cuss* each other in their own language.

The Bible tells us, "And I say unto you, Ask, and it shall be given you; seek, and ye shall find; knock, and it shall be opened unto you. For every one that asketh receiveth; and he that seeketh findeth; and to him that knocketh it shall be opened. If a son shall ask bread of any of you that is a father, will he give him a stone? or if he ask a fish, will he for a fish give him a serpent? Or if he

Invoke A Blessing On Yourself.

shall ask an egg, will he offer him a scorpion? If ye then, being evil, know how to give good gifts unto your children: how much more shall your heavenly Father give the Holy Spirit to them that ask Him?" (Luke 11:9-13).

Pray to The Father in The Name of Jesus. After you finish the prayer, keep moving your lips. Nothing will come out if you keep your mouth shut.

Pray This Prayer To Receive The Gift...

"Father God, I am a believer. I am Your child and You are my Father. I have accepted Jesus as my Savior. He is my Lord. I believe Your Word with all my heart and I believe that Your Word is the truth.

"Your Word says that if I will ask, You will give me The Gift of The Holy Spirit with the evidence of speaking in tongues. In The Name of Jesus Christ, my Lord, I am asking you to fill me with Your Precious Holy Spirit.

"Father, baptize me in The Holy Spirit.

"Because of Your Word, I believe that I now receive it and I thank You for this Gift. I believe that The Holy Spirit is within me and by Faith I accept it.

Now, Holy Spirit, rise up within me as I praise The Father. I fully expect to speak with other tongues

Invoke A Blessing On Yourself.

as You give me the utterance. I receive it in the strong Name of Jesus of Nazareth… "

The More You Pray In Tongues…The More Comfortable You Will Become.

Use The Gift. *Practice*.

God will not *force* you to speak in tongues.

The Holy Spirit will *supply* the words, but you have to supply the *sound*. Nowhere, in The Bible does it say that The Holy Spirit did the speaking. "And they were filled with the Holy Ghost, and began to speak with other tongues, as the Holy Spirit gave them Utterance," (Acts 2:4).

Invoke A Blessing On Yourself.

Contact Us.

If The Holy Spirit is leading you to sow a seed into Invoke A Blessing Ministry please do so.
We tithe and sow because we believe in the harvest, so your seed will be used as indicated.

If this book had an impact on your life please write me so others can be encouraged thru your testimony. You may email me at: info@InvokeABlessing.com

You may want to sow a seed or purchase another copy of my book by going to: www.InvokeABlessing.com

You may follow me on Facebook and Twitter.

Please let me know if you want me to come and speak at your church or organization.

Please let us know if you see any errors in the book, because we are striving for perfection and excellence.

Invoke A Blessing On Yourself.

You may send us your seed and your letters
Please circle:
Check Money Order AmEx Discover Master Card Visa

Credit Card #_____

Exp. ___/_____ Signature _____

Name _____

Birth Date ___/_____

Address _____

City _____ State _____

Phone _____

Email _____

Your Seed of Faith Offerings will be used to support Invoke A Blessing Ministry. Invoke A Blessing Ministry reserves the right to redirect funds as needed to carry out our charitable purpose. When Invoke A Blessing Ministry receives more funds for a project than needed, the excess will be used for another worthy outreach.

Invoke A Blessing Ministry
P.O. Box 163772
Ft. Worth, TX 76161-3772

www.ingramcontent.com/pod-product-compliance
Lightning Source LLC
Chambersburg PA
CBHW051424290426
44109CB00016B/1424